You've Got
Style

*Your personal guide
for relating to others*

Robert A. Rohm, Ph.D.

Personality
INSIGHTS

Editor – Beth Mc Lendon
Layout and Graphics – Pedro Gonzalez

Credits:
Photos of Dr. Robert A. Rohm by Rick Diamond

ISBN 0-9641080-7-0
Printed in the United States of America

This book is lovingly dedicated to the
Personality Insights Team

Robert A. Rohm, Ph.D.

For over 30 years, Dr. Robert A. Rohm has affected people's lives through speaking, teaching and encouraging individuals across the United States, Canada, Europe and Asia. Drawing on his earned doctorate from the University of North Texas in Higher Education Administration and Counseling, he speaks to audiences on personal development and business relationships. His special mix of humor, stories and illustrations relate to old and young from all walks of life. Millions have laughed and learned from Dr. Rohm.

A dynamic speaker, Dr. Rohm has entertained and enlightened audiences as large as 70,000 people, and he has shared the platform with other great speakers like Zig Ziglar, Les Brown, President George Bush Sr., Rush Limbaugh, Charles "Tremendous" Jones, Peter Lowe, Lou Holtz and Joe Theisman. He has spoken to audiences with celebrities including Tricia Yearwood, Johnny Cash, Glen Campbell, Howie Mandel, Miss America Heather Whitestone and Dionne Warwick.

Dr. Rohm has authored or co-authored several books including *Positive Personality Profiles, Who Do You Think You Are, Anyway?* and *Sponsor With Style.* As a training company, Personality Insights, Inc., draws upon Dr. Rohm's unique presentation style for its resource materials, videotapes, audiotapes and CDs to empower families to improve their relationships at home and to empower co-workers to increase the effectiveness of their teams at work.

Table of Contents

Foreword

In today's busy society with its frantic demands and expectations, as well as hope-filled opportunities, sometimes it is easy for us to think that we could accomplish so much more... if only other people we had to interact with were not so difficult to deal with. Have you ever had the thought, "It would be so much easier for me to cope with all of life's demands if only other people felt, thought, and acted like me"?

Unfortunately, the world is not made up of cookie-cutter clusters of people who are perfect and predictable. Although members of the human race do share some universal traits, needs, desires, and drives, each one of us is still unique... and special! There is not a wonderful one-size-fits-all solution for coping with people with whom we associate in our personal and professional lives on a daily basis.

Every now and then we are afforded insights and wisdom into the "interpersonal puzzles" that we call family, friends, peers, and fellow colleagues. You hold in your hands one of the greatest keys to unlocking the mystery of that puzzle we call *people*. Dr. Robert A. Rohm has over thirty years of insightful experience and wisdom which he shares with clarity to help us understand ourselves, as well as others, so that we can successfully get along and interact with people. Once we understand "what makes us tick" and the different elements that make you uniquely *you*, you can begin to understand what makes others the way *they* are.

We cannot change other people, but we can change our perceptions of other peoples' personality styles and how to better relate to them. *You've Got Style* will set you on the path to successful communication and healthy, successful relationships in all the realms of your personal and professional lives. As Dr. Rohm says, "If I understand you and you understand me, doesn't it stand to reason that we will be in a position to have a better relationship?"

You are in for a real treat that will profit you throughout life as you begin to better understand yourself and others as you explore these principles of personality styles! Happy exploring!

Dexter Yager

Chapter One

Finding Your Style

Years ago, scientists and philosophers began to recognize that the differences in people's behavior seemed to follow a pattern. They observed the personalities of people and described the behavior they saw. The D-I-S-C Model of Human Behavior is a result of their efforts. We can use it to increase our awareness and to understand why we think, feel and act as we do.

Personality Types

There are four basic personality types, also known as temperaments. The four types are like four quadrants, or four parts, of a circle. These four basic personality types make up four parts of an individual personality style. These parts are interrelated in fascinating ways - combining in multiple patterns. No individual's unique personality is totally defined, or influenced, by only one set of characteristics or traits. The different ways in which the traits from each of the four basic types blend together make up each person's distinct personality style. In fact, it is the limitless blending of these elements that accounts for the great diversity and uniqueness of personalities. It is what makes each person unique and special! To understand this concept, let's begin with two different ways to divide our circle. This will help give us two different ways to describe your personality style using two simple classifications or distinctions.

Are You Outgoing or Reserved?

Outgoing people are more active and optimistic. Reserved people are more passive and cautious. One disposition is not better than the other. They are simply different, and both are important.

Outgoing People

There are several ways that we can describe outgoing, fast-paced people. They love to go and do things. They seem to be excited or in a hurry most of the time. A crowd does not easily intimidate them, because they love to be in the middle of whatever is happening! If a friend calls to ask, "Would you like to go to...," they have heard all they need to hear, and the answer is "Yes!" They thrive on doing many things at the same time. Rather than look for excitement, they create it. They don't have to go to the party...they *are* the party! They do not hesitate to jump into the pool of life feet first!

They are optimistic and positive. They look for the diamond in every lump of coal or the gold in every clump of dirt. They expect things to turn out well or at least to be able to make things turn out well. Generally, they expect to win, and often they win with flair. Outward appearance and actions are usually more important to them than inward qualities and thoughts. They see the big picture and do not concentrate on details.

They are usually involved in community projects, civic clubs, church groups and all kinds of organizations where they often hold leadership positions. They like being in charge of things, not because they do the most work, but because they like to tell others what to do! They are enthusiastic, so people like to put them in charge. When you eat a meal with these people, you may find that you are still enjoying your salad when they are asking for the dessert menu! They really believe that if a little is good, then more must be better! They have to learn that just enough may be just a little bit instead of a lot!

This type of person is energetic. They often plan to do more than they can do. They usually talk faster, work harder and get others to help so that they get to their desired results in the end. They can echo the words of General George S. Patton who said, "Lead me, follow me or get out of my way!"

Reserved People

There are several ways to depict a person who is more reserved or slower-paced. They do not jump into the pool of life but prefer to test the waters first. After all, who knows how cold the water is! They simply hold back. They do not speak as freely, or as quickly, as more outgoing individuals. However, this is not from a lack of interest. When they do speak, you will want to listen!

They may be like the proverbial tortoise who was left in the dust by the outgoing, fast-paced rabbit. But just like in the fable, they can cross the finish line ahead of those who started the race in a flash. They may be slower-paced, but they have patience and stamina to get the job done. This poem shares an important secret about these individuals:

> *Life's battles don't always go*
> *To the stronger or faster man*
> *But sooner or later the one who wins*
> *Is the one who thinks he can.*

Reserved individuals are concerned about the details of a situation before doing something, because they do not like to be surprised. They would prefer to have a safe plan rather than take things as they come. They are cautious and a little reluctant to get involved in too many activities. They tend to be more passive and content to watch the game instead of actually playing it.

Reserved, or slower-paced, individuals are analytical and discerning. They concentrate on foundations and underlying details, not just on the big picture and outward appearances. These traits help them to see the reality of a situation very quickly. To these people, quality and substance are important.

They prefer to operate behind the scenes by getting the job done and making sure everything is handled correctly. They have more difficulty starting a conversation with a stranger than a more outgoing person, but what they share is worth the wait. They would rather have one or two close friends than have a crowd of acquaintances around them.

Your Motor Activity

Let's illustrate these two types of people. Each of us has an "internal motor" that drives us. It has a fast pace that makes us more Outgoing, or it has a slow pace that makes us more Reserved. In the illustration below, we have divided our circle with a horizontal line. The arrows indicate that the darker shading, closer to each tip, indicates more intensity in that trait, while the lighter shading, closer to the midline, shows less intensity in this motor activity. You may be extremely outgoing or reserved, or you may be just moderately outgoing or reserved. (Remember, your personality style is also influenced by your environment. Therefore, depending upon

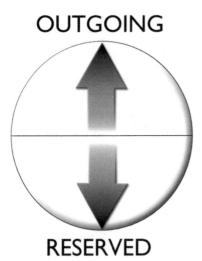

your environment, at times, you may be influenced to be more outgoing and at other times more reserved. For the sake of this illustration, however, just know that in general you tend to be either more outgoing or more reserved.)

You have probably identified more closely with one side or the other side of this circle. No matter which side of the circle is more comfortable for you, you can see that both types are valuable. They are different, and we need both types. We need outgoing, fast-paced people to get things going and get people excited. Although this is their natural approach, they can become aware of the need for balance in their own personality style and then learn how to be more steady and cautious. We need reserved, slower-paced people to take care of details and to be thoughtful of people. These reserved people can become aware of the need for balance in their own personality style and learn how to be more demanding and inspiring.

Are You Task-Oriented or People-Oriented?

We can also cut our circle in half the other way vertically, representing two more distinct classifications of human personality. Some people are more task-oriented, while others are more people-oriented.

Task-oriented individuals enjoy doing things like making plans and working on projects. People-oriented individuals love to interact with other people and enjoy conversation while developing close friendships.

Task-Oriented People

Task-oriented people find great pleasure in a job well done. We like to call them *high tech*. They focus on function. They like to make things work, so they love using technology. To this type, nothing is better than a fine-tuned, well-oiled, peak-performing machine. They talk about form and function. They want people and things to be in the best form and the best shape to perform the task at hand. They love online banking, because they can access their balance at a moment's notice. They do not just talk about it, but they actually use this and other new forms of technology! They may still keep their own running balance in their head, or on paper, but they love this form of convenience. They enjoy checking the bank and having access to their financial information at all times of the day or night.

These people are great at working on projects. They can really get into the process of seeing a job take shape and then watching it get accomplished. They are excellent planners who can see the end of a project from the beginning. They are the ones who put together plans that work! They agree with Ralph Waldo Emerson when he wrote, "What I must do is all that concerns me, not what the people think."

How might a task-oriented person approach a task? If you watch him rake his yard on a Saturday morning, you might observe him first coming out with a rake and looking the yard over like a field marshal preparing the battle plans. Then, he rakes one section of the yard at a time, completing the job as efficiently as possible.

Imagine that his more people-oriented neighbor is out taking a nice, leisurely Saturday morning stroll. When the two friends see each other, the one who is raking the yard responds with a quick, "Hi!" However, he does not miss a stroke. He simply keeps raking as he secretly thinks, "Oh, no, I hope my neighbor doesn't stop to talk my ear off. I'm not out here to visit. I'm here to rake!" Should the unsuspecting neighbor continue to talk, he may find himself interrupted by his friend with the rake who says, "Excuse me; I'll be right back." Do you know where he is going? Yes, he is going into the garage to get another rake for his friend! He thinks to himself, "Two can rake better than one. If he wants to talk, I would be happy to listen, as long as I can get this job done." The task-oriented person also enjoys talking, but he has to get his work done. That is just the way he is wired.

People-Oriented People

Our people-oriented friends are very different. They are more interested in relationships with other people than in accomplishing a task. These people seem to be more emotional and more caring. They love talking and sharing feelings together. They just love to be with people.

Imagine now that a people-oriented neighbor needs to rake his yard. This person is more concerned about the feelings of other people, so he will handle the Saturday morning yard work very differently from a task-oriented person. Rather than being driven to complete the task, he will begin the project, because he is concerned with what the neighbors might think if the yard looks bad. He feels compelled to rake the yard, so that his neighbors will like him and be happy with him. He has a strong awareness of the needs and desires of people.

If someone walked by and stopped to talk to him while he was raking, he would smile and think, "This is great! I love talking with this neighbor!" Then he would probably say, "Why don't we go into the house, have a cup of coffee and visit? I didn't want to rake the yard now, anyway! I can finish that later." Such is the nature of the people-oriented personality. Life is all about enjoying friendships with people.

Your Compass Activity

Let's illustrate this concept. Just as we have a motor that drives us, we also have a compass that draws us toward either tasks or people.Because we are drawn toward either tasks or people, we are either task-oriented or people-oriented. In the illustration to the right, the 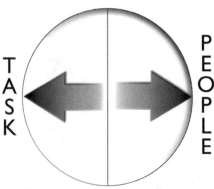 arrows indicate that the lighter shading, closer to the midline, shows less intensity in this compass activity, while the darker shading, towards each tip, reveals more intensity in each activity. You may be extremely people-oriented or task-oriented, or you may be just moderately people-oriented or task-oriented.

You have probably identified more closely with one or the other side of this circle. No matter which side of the circle is more comfortable for you, you can see that both types are valuable, and they are simply different. We need both types! We need task-oriented people to get our work planned and completed. Although this is their natural approach, they can become aware of the need for balance in their own personality style by learning how to be more conversational and to consider the feelings of others. We need people-oriented types to get everyone involved and to make each one feel more comfortable. They can become aware of the need for balance in their own personality style by learning how to plan their work and then work their plan.

Putting It All Together

When we put together both the motor activity of the outgoing and reserved types with the compass activity for the task and people-oriented types, we can see the four-quadrant Model of Human Behavior illustrated on the following page.

We see that:

THE D TYPE IS OUTGOING AND TASK-ORIENTED
THE I TYPE IS OUTGOING AND PEOPLE-ORIENTED
THE S TYPE IS RESERVED AND PEOPLE-ORIENTED
THE C TYPE IS RESERVED AND TASK-ORIENTED

In Review

D Type

OUTGOING

T
A
S
K

The **D** is in the top half of the circle, which is the outgoing half, and it is on the left side, which is the task-oriented side. Thus, the **D** type personality is outgoing and task-oriented.

I Type

OUTGOING

P
E
O
P
L
E

The **I** is in the top half of the circle, which is the outgoing half, and it is on the right side, which is the people-oriented side. Thus, the **I** type personality is outgoing and people-oriented.

Both **D**s and **I**s are active and outgoing, but they go and do in different directions. The **D**, being task-oriented, has a strong desire to direct many people's activities to get a certain job completed. The **I**, being people-oriented, wants to look good in front of people. An **I** desires status and prestige.

S Type

The **S** is in the bottom half of the circle, which is the reserved half, and it is on the right side, which is the people-oriented side. Thus, the **S** type personality is reserved and people-oriented.

C Type

The **C** is in the bottom half of the circle, which is the reserved half, and it is on the left, which is the task-oriented side. Thus, the **C** type personality is reserved and task-oriented.

Both **S**s and **C**s are reserved, but they have a different orientation. The **S**, being people-oriented, has a strong desire to please people and make everyone comfortable. The **C**, being task-oriented, wants to focus on his or her plans and procedures for getting the job done.

Remember, all four types have an important perspective to offer us. One type isn't better than another. With this model, we are not looking for right and wrong, or good and bad behavior. Each behavior type is important to consider in any situation. Each type has behavior that is effective and appropriate in some settings. We are exploring the differences in personality styles, so that we can better understand ourselves and others.

What does **DISC** mean?

The letters in the four quadrants are significant, because they are your keys to remembering the **DISC** Model of Human Behavior. As we look at these four quadrants of the circle together, we are able to visualize the **DISC** model. Each of us is a unique blend of these four parts. Let's introduce the symbol and color for each **DISC** type now:

The **D** Type

We use an exclamation point to depict the **D** type, because the **D** type is emphatic in everything! You will notice that the **D** is in the upper left quadrant of the circle. The exclamation point in the logo on the back cover of this book is green. Green is our color for the **D** type, because like a green light, it means GO! Six key traits, or characteristics, describe the outgoing and task-oriented **D** type: **D**ominant, **D**irect, **D**emanding, **D**ecisive, **D**etermined and a **D**oer. Chapter Two is devoted to the powerful **D** type, so we can look forward to that discussion.

The **I** Type

We use a star to depict the **I** type, because the **I** type loves to be the star of the show! You will notice that the **I** is in the upper right quadrant of the circle. The star in the logo on the back cover of this book is red. Red is our color for the **I** type, because it is fiery and exciting and shouts *stop and watch me!* Six key traits, or characteristics, describe the outgoing and people-oriented **I** type: **I**nspiring, **I**nfluencing, **I**mpressionable, **I**nteractive, **I**mpressive and **I**nvolved. Chapter Three is devoted to the people-loving **I** type, so we can look forward to that discussion.

The S Type

We use a plus or minus sign to depict the S type, because Ss are flexible and willing to respond, more or less, the way you might ask them to! You will notice that the S is in the lower right quadrant of the circle. The plus or minus sign in the logo on the back cover of this book is blue. Blue is our color for the S type, because it is a peaceful, harmonious color, just like the color of the sky. Six key traits, or characteristics, describe the reserved and people-oriented S type: Supportive, Stable, Steady, Sweet, Status quo and Shy. Chapter Four is devoted to the predictable S type, so we can look forward to that discussion.

The C Type

We use a question mark to depict the C type, because the C type loves to question everything! You will notice that the C is in the lower left quadrant of the circle. The question mark in the logo on the back cover of this book is yellow. Yellow is our color for the C type, because it means caution, like the yellow in a traffic light. It also reminds us of the radiant energy of the sun, so it pictures the intensity of the C type. Six key traits, or characteristics, describe the reserved and task-oriented C type: Cautious, Calculating, Competent, Conscientious, Contemplative and Careful. Chapter Five is devoted to the correct C type, so we can look forward to that discussion.

Getting the Keys

So far, we have presented the keys of the **DISC** Model of Human Behavior. In the following chapters, we will explore each type more closely. You will see that each type is different, and each type is very special. As you think more about the traits of each type, you may be aware that you really identify most with one or two of these types.

Most people are predominantly strong in two or sometimes three types. However, you may only relate to just one of the traits. And, in addition to that, you may feel that you really do not understand one of the types at all. This is perfectly natural, for while we all have some of all four types within us, we usually have only one or two high types, and one or two low types. The payoff for learning about our low types is invaluable, because this is the place where you can learn and grow in your own personal life. It is also a great opportunity to learn about someone close to you.

You've Got Style! You have a special personality style that includes characteristics, or traits, from all four classic **DISC** types. Your personality style is colorful, just like the colorful logo on the back cover of this book. Let's explore how each **DISC** type colors your unique personality style!

Chapter Two

Introducing
the Dominant Type

Whoever said, "When the going gets tough, the tough get going!" was really describing a Dominant, high D type! They identify with the color green. To them it means a green light- Go!, the color of growing things and the power of money. They are self-starters who know how to make things happen. Their natural self-composure makes them confident and sure of themselves, so they can be very convincing when they want you to do something for them! A high D will start the ball rolling in a straightforward manner and will exert control to get things done. This outgoing and task-oriented D type is highly competitive. Life is a game with a series of challenges, and they plan to win it! They love to play any game that they can win. After all, to them winning is what any game is all about!

Put Dominant types in a challenging situation, and they are in their element. Their approach will be very determined. They are decisive and do not mind taking a risk on the way to accomplishing their goals. A high D once said, "But you don't understand! If it wasn't impossible, it wouldn't be fun to do!"

Sky diving and scuba diving are sports they love, because they are adventuresome by nature. They want to fly higher, run faster, dive deeper and do what has never been done before! Theirs is the pioneering spirit. A tough assignment, stiff competition or pressure situations invigorate high Ds. Their forceful approach will overcome all obstacles.

Perhaps more than any other type, high Ds seek an activity where they can be in charge. Directing the efforts of everyone involved is their talent, so they are dynamic leaders. They never say, "Die." They would rather say, "If at first you don't succeed, try, try again!" They are ambitious and will do more than you ask if they can beat the competition with extra effort. Ds are drivers and doers. They make the world go around. They are movers and shakers. They have things to do, places to go and people to see. If you work or play with **D**s… you had better keep up, because they won't wait for you!

Don't expect too much sympathy from **D**s. They naturally feel that needing sympathy is a sign of weakness. They don't want to be perceived as weak, and they assume that you don't either! They don't express a lot of warmth or empathy. They'll be quick to declare, "Welcome to the real world! Now grow up, and get to work!" They are direct in their approach to problems, and this really shows in what they say. They may seem harsh when speaking bluntly, but they simply want to get to the bottom line as quickly as possible. High **D**s are very **D**emanding, both from themselves and others. They seldom take no for an answer. No to them simply means ask again later! If you stick to your no, they will be thinking of a way to go around you.

They do not mean to be overbearing — they just have so much **D**rive and **D**etermination that they want to keep going. They are unafraid to stand alone. They are **D**etermined to move ahead and achieve victory! If you ask high **D**s what they think, you can count on them to tell you. They will usually outline something they want to do and assess the problems they face. High **D**s look at difficulties and problems as temporary setbacks, so they don't hold grudges as long as progress is being made. They focus on the goal, and would prefer to forget about the details. They are naturally dominant and have a commanding presence that makes them say,

> *"Get the job done — just do it! Overcome opposition, and achieve your goals! Winners never quit, and quitters never win!"*

Strengths of the Dominant Type

All four **DISC** types have wonderful qualities that bring so much richness and diversity to our world. While we recognize that each of us has a natural personality perspective, we also recognize that each of us makes daily choices about the way in which we will behave. We can become aware that it is most often our strengths pushed to an extreme that cause us the most difficulties in life. This next section can help **D**ominant people to recognize the strengths of their behavior under control, and see how struggles occur as those strengths are pushed out of control.

COURAGEOUS ....can become Reckless

High **D**s will gladly take on a challenge and do what it takes to get the job done, no matter what they must do. They will persevere in the face of adversity, being *courageous*, while others may feel defeated and want to quit. Not afraid to take a risk, they will make even an unpopular decision when it must be made and will convince others to follow. John F. Kennedy expressed this high **D** attitude in his book, *Profiles in Courage*, when he wrote,

> *In whatever arena of life one may meet the challenge of courage, whatever may be the sacrifices he faces if he follows his conscience - the loss of his friends, his fortune, his contentment, even the esteem of his fellow men - each man must decide for himself the course he will follow.*

However, when pushed to an extreme and out of control, they can become *reckless*. They do or say things to accomplish their goals that may cause hurt that might have been avoided with a little patience or sensitivity towards the people involved. They must learn to remember that hurting those people can keep them from being able to accomplish future goals or cause others to abandon their leadership.

QUICK TO RESPOND......can become Rude

Ask **D**s a question, and they may answer you before you finish the question. Under control, they are *quick to respond* directly and to-the-point. Out of control, **D**s may come across as *rude,* because they push past the small talk and confront the real issues directly.

Others may find their quickness to respond overbearing and

offensive, when they never mean to give that impression. They must learn to respect the feelings of others; then their deliberate and direct approach can keep emotions in check and build self-confidence in those around them.

GOAL-ORIENTED......can become Impatient

They not only set *goals* – they achieve them! Once high **D**s make up their mind to do something, they drive for the goal. If the goal seems more difficult than they expected or is taking others too much time to achieve, they can become *impatient*. Taking control through leadership is a natural part of their style, so they may become impatient and may assume leadership roles before they are actually offered or earned. High **D**s are energetic goal seekers who choose to work with people, so that they can bring others with them to the goal!

RESULTS-ORIENTED......can become Pushy

The task orientation of **D**s will keep them very focused on getting the *results* they desire. And results are important! It is difficult to measure intent, desire or excitement, but anyone can measure results! High **D**s need to remember that others may not share their drive. If they become *pushy*, they will create resistance from the very same people who could help them to achieve their results. They must understand that winning at any cost may cost them relationships with people in ways that they will later regret. High **D**s can appreciate their own self-motivation and seek to lead in ways that allow others to motivate themselves.

DELIBERATE.........can become Dictatorial

Ds do things very *deliberately* and must have a purpose for doing anything. They enjoy planning their goals and strategies to find the fastest way to achieve them. They are sure that their plans will work. In their determination, they can quickly become *dictatorial* by forcing people to fit into their plans and failing to listen to the input of others. People may withdraw from working with them and the high **D**s will not understand why. When this happens, the **D**ominant person has the opportunity to learn that negotiation is more powerful than coercion and that working *with* people is better than having those same people work *against* him or her.

SELF-CONFIDENT...can become Conceited

High **D**s believe they can overcome any barrier or solve any problem. This *confidence* sustains them as they work through the problems that inevitably occur on their way to success. Becoming successful too easily or quickly may let high **D**s become *conceited* and give the impression that they have all the answers. People often just quietly walk away from them, because they feel that high **D**s don't need them or that they care only for their own high **D** plans. **D**ominant people must realize that, while they know that they can do great things, they can do so much more when other people help them.

DIRECT..................can become Offensive

You will always know exactly where you stand with **D**s! They say what they mean, and mean what they say. As they deal with people, they will be *direct* to deal with a problem instead of holding a grudge. When a difficult or complicated situation needs to be handled with sensitivity, their directness can feel *offensive* and may alienate the people involved. They might consider how their own words would offend if they could hear themselves. Understanding personality styles can help them to appreciate how saying the same thing in a different way can make all of the difference in how it is received.

SELF-RELIANT..........can become Arrogant

Ds take care of themselves and will *rely* first on themselves to get the results they want. They challenge others by their example. **D**s instill confidence in others to believe in themselves and accomplish their goals. They echo the words of Napoleon, "Circumstances? I make circumstances!"

When **D**s are out of control, they become *arrogant*. They think that they can do just about anything, and that they can do it alone! Others may feel the burn of their arrogance when **D**s blame others for their own shortcomings. They will do well to remember that they are imperfect people, just like the rest of us.

STRAIGHTFORWARD...can become Abrasive

What you see is what you get with high **D**s. They clearly tell you in a *straightforward* manner about the situation and what they want to accomplish. High **D**s would agree with Sir Winston Churchill who said, "If you have a point to make, don't try to be subtle or clever. Use a pile driver. Hit the point once. Then come back, and hit it again. Then hit it a third time with a tremendous whack." Because the goal is so important to them, they discount their own feelings in a situation and can just as easily discount the feelings of others and become *abrasive* to people. They expect people to choose to feel how they have chosen to feel. They need to learn to be considerate of others: realize that others feel differently, and respect those feelings. High **D**s will benefit from the better relationships that this respect will build for them.

COMPETITIVE ....can become Ruthless

Ds love to make anything a game that they can win! They see competition as a natural motivation to do better. In any endeavor, their *competitive* spirit will spur them on. They want to win more than anything and may abandon their team if it does not perform. When they become *ruthless*, in order to win, they hurt many people. **D**s are unaware that they are hurting themselves in the long run.

They must learn the meaning of their Secret Tip:

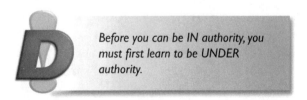

Before you can be IN authority, you must first learn to be UNDER authority.

Attitudes and Preferences of the Dominant Type

The exclamation point represents the power of this style! They are demanding, first of themselves, and then of others. We can admire their boldness and willingness to tackle difficult tasks. **D**s are **D**irect. They say what they mean and mean what they say.

The **D**ominant type would say,

"I like a challenge! Something that may be fun for you is boring to me, if there is no point or purpose in it for me. Give me the tough issues, because I can deal with them. You see, I really don't like conversations that are purely social and without any real purpose. I love a heated debate, because it empowers me to make quick decisions. Please don't give me routine tasks. Inventing new ways to do things is much more to my liking. In fact, when you give me a job to do, don't restrict me to one workplace and don't expect me to be responsible for minor details. I really like to be doing several things at once, and I will quit a job if it doesn't hold the challenge that I need. I work at a fast pace, and I perform better if there is competition or a deadline involved. I make things work, but I like to get expert opinions instead of doing projects that require long-term critical analysis. Enough talk — let's get to work!"

People You Know from the Dominant Type

Research indicates that only about 10% of the general population have this **D**ominant type profile. It is the smallest **DISC** group, but they are powerful enough to leave their mark on the world! As you have read this chapter, you, no doubt, have thought of friends and relatives with this style. There is a natural correlation between a job or role, and the person who fills it. As you can imagine, **D**ominant types make excellent producers, leaders and builders in any field. They make great coaches and military officers. They become good law enforcement agents and political leaders. They develop into fine entrepreneurs, business owners and corporate presidents. They make good dictators! Their profession or role in life may vary, but their personality will not. It will be churning inside them to go and grow, to move and shake, and to advance to bigger and better horizons. They are never satisfied with the status quo. They are constantly looking for better ideas and bigger ways of doing things.

In A Dominant Style...

"I tried being reasonable:
I didn't like it."

— Clint Eastwood

"The truth of the matter is that you always know the right thing to do. The hard part is doing it."

— General Norman Swartzkopf

"No one can make you feel inferior without your consent."

— Eleanor Roosevelt

"I don't think anything is unrealistic
if you believe you can do it."
— Mike Ditka

"Don't spend time beating on a wall,
hoping to transform it into a door."
— Dr. Laura Schlessinger

"Security is mostly a superstition.
It does not exist in nature.
...life is either a daring adventure or nothing."
— Helen Keller

"Eagles don't flock.
You have to find them one at a time."
— Ross Perot

"I was the kind nobody thought would make it.
I had a funny Boston accent.
I couldn't pronounce my Rs.
I wasn't a beauty."
— Barbara Walters

"I don't measure a man's success
by how high he climbs
but how high he bounces
when he hits bottom."
— General George S. Patton

"You'll always miss 100% of the shots you don't take."
— Wayne Gretsky

"I'm the boss, applesauce!"
- Judge Judy

The Dominant Type in Review

As we have defined and described the high **D** type, you may have found many descriptions that fit you. If so, we would say that you have a high **D** personality style. On the other hand, you may feel that this chapter describes someone very different from you. In that case, we would say that you have a low **D** personality style. For an individual assessment of your personality style, the *Adult Profile Assessment* enables you to explore how the **D**ominant type is part of your personality style. (Call our office, or visit our web site to place an order.)

We are attracted to the **D**ominant type, because they are dynamic leaders who love to be in charge. Powerful and ambitious, they drive toward their goals. They are undaunted by difficulty or opposition and thrive on challenges. Conflict seems to energize them. If they find themselves in a static environment, watch out! They will pick up the pace, stir up the mix and get things moving! They seek an environment that includes new challenges and freedom from supervision, because they live to make choices that will solve problems. Their underlying priority in any decision is power. They exercise power in making decisions in order to solve problems and achieve their goals. When under control, high **D**s are powerful and forceful. **D**s are able to bring to reality what others may feel is an impossible dream.

We all need people with the **D**ominant style in our lives!

Chapter Three

Introducing
the Inspiring Type

The *I*nspiring, high *I* type loves being with people! Whether with one person, or a large crowd, this type thrives on contact with others... and the more, the better! *I*s identify with the color red, for to them it is fiery and exciting! They want others to see a red light that says, "Stop, and watch me!" People do stop, and watch. People enjoy being with them, because they are always so hopeful. Things may seem sad for the moment, but the *I*nspiring type is always hopeful and sure that tomorrow will be a better day. Social and charming, tomorrow will be a better day if you spend it with them! When you are with them, you feel fine. To them, all of life is a good time. They help you have a wonderful experience every time you are together. After all, they love to be on top of the world!

In just a few minutes, a high *I* can meet a total stranger and make him or her feel right at home. *I*s are friendly and carefree, and their generous nature allows them to focus all their attention on this newfound friend. You see, there are no strangers to high *I*s. They are simply friends that this interactive person has not yet met! They usually enjoy a wide range of social relationships from many different backgrounds. Their optimistic attitude makes them fun to be with, and their happy disposition helps them get along with almost everyone.

High *I*s like to be right in the heart of what everyone is doing. They are involved in many organizations, clubs and groups, in which prestige or personal recognition is offered. They enjoy being in front of a group. High *I* types are so *I*nfluencing they can sell snowballs to snowmen. They make everything sound fantastic and often exhibit more confidence than ability. They are so enthusiastic and expressive that they may innocently make things sound better than they actually are! They project a polished image. Being keenly aware of their appearance to others, they are usually quite *I*mpressive.

Because they are good talkers, they can make you believe almost anything. If they are honest, they can become inspiring leaders. If not, they make great con artists. They love to persuade people. They love the art of the deal. It has been said that a salesman is most easily sold. This must have been written about the *I*nspiring type, for they are naturally trusting souls who are very *I*mpressionable, accepting what others tell them openly and without suspicion. This can cause them trouble, because they are also *I*mpulsive. They are prone to jump into the pool of life when it sounds like fun, or they are in the mood. And jump in they do - sometimes crashing into the hard cement of the empty pool bottom when they haven't tested the waters first. Unfortunately, they usually only face reality when reality hits them in the face! This is why I often love to say that high *I*s can be higher than a kite or lower than a skunk. But they do not stay low very long, for they soon find another exciting party to enjoy!

I types are stimulating. They feel best when exciting things are happening. They love to stir things up and get the party going! Calmness is not a part of their makeup. They are naturally magnetic, attracting a group of people to themselves. High *I*s are the life of the party! High *I*s are politicians in the best sense of the word. They are light-hearted and friendly, so people are drawn to them. When they feel strongly about something (and they usually feel strongly about things), they can express their feelings so strikingly that they are highly persuasive. We really want to believe them, because they are so attractive to us, and they make us feel so good about life. They love to make things fun. I jokingly say, "They have all their marbles, but their *shooter* is missing!" Like Peter Pan, they don't want to grow up but want to enjoy every moment in life as a great adventure. They would love for you to come along with them, and you can almost hear them say,

> *"I am for you! We can have fun, and if we all pull in the same direction, our success will never end!"*

Strengths of the Inspiring Type

All four **DISC** types have wonderful qualities that bring so much richness and diversity into our world. While we recognize that each of us has a natural personality perspective, we also recognize that all of us make daily choices about the way in which we will behave. We can become aware that it is most often our strengths pushed to an extreme that cause us the most disappointment in life. This next section can help *I*nspiring people to recognize the strengths of their behavior under control, and see how struggles occur as those strengths are pushed out of control.

OPTIMISTIC ....can become Unrealistic

They are just so happy to be here! Life for them is one long party just waiting to happen, and they can't wait for you to come along! They expect everything to be wonderful and exciting, and they see themselves as the star of the show. *I*nspiring types know that things may look gray today, but they sing along with Little Orphan Annie, "If we just hold on... the sun will come out tomorrow!" Their *optimism* is contagious, so they really encourage everyone around them through difficult times. Unfortunately, sometimes optimism is not enough. Pushed to an extreme, high *I*s can refuse to face reality, and will often become *unrealistic*. As their optimism gets extreme, they can lose credibility with others. They may ignore facts which are essential to a situation and its potential results. When they cannot see the facts because of their intense feelings, then instead of things being happy, fun and exciting, they can be surprised with bitter disappointment. They learn, from experience, how the hard facts and complexities of a problem cannot always be wished away.

PERSUASIVE.......can become Manipulative

They are engaging storytellers who love talking about the fascinating people they have known. It is simply amazing how many people they have met! When they are trying to *persuade* a person to their point of view, they use their talent for drawing interesting examples from many sources for their illustrations. They can draw many people into their opinion in this way. However, if their stories bend the facts too far, others will feel that they are *manipulative* - simply trying to get others to do what benefits them. This manipulation can cause deep resentment and seriously damage their personal relationships. Learning to listen to others is not easy for the *I*nspiring type, but listening can help them to learn from and build lasting relationships with others.

EXCITED...............can become Emotional

They are so *excited*, and their excitement is infectious! When high *I*s are leading, their enthusiasm will attract and energize people! They make work so much fun that achieving great goals seems possible, even worth trying to reach! Sometimes they face disapproval or public embarrassment, because, in their excitement, they promise what they will not deliver. When this happens, they can become *emotional* and explode with an unexpected personal attack. They can become more consistent, and, therefore, more credible if they make themselves accountable to someone. This friend can help them remember to do what they said they would do when they were excited enough to make a commitment in the first place.

COMMUNICATIVE......can become Gossipy

They don't hesitate to *communicate* almost anything to anyone! How easily high *I*s can start a conversation or explain their point of view! Most people find it easy to listen to them and enjoy being around them. People are attracted to them for encouragement and coaching. Because they like to talk and share what they know and whom they know, they can be *gossipy*. They share private information without meaning to hurt others. This may easily wound those involved and cause division in their family or group of friends. High *I*s can learn to recognize privileged information and begin to protect other people through a silence that honors them.

SPONTANEOUS........can become Impulsive

Life would be much less fun without the spontaneity of high *I*s. They are always ready to walk through the door of opportunity that can lead to exciting and unexpected results. They would agree with Boris Pasternak in saying, "Surprise is the greatest gift which life can grant us." However, out of control, their *spontaneous* nature can become *impulsive*. They can burn up their energy on one very important idea, and then jump to another incredible opportunity without producing any tangible results. Learning to use short-term goals can help them to stick with something when the initial excitement has worn thin.

OUTGOING............can become Unfocused

The *outgoing I* will go to a party and know everyone there before he or she leaves. The *I*nspiring type has a gift for meeting people. *I*s naturally just "reach out and touch someone." They have the wonderful ability to set people at ease, often through the humor they find in any situation. Only a high *I* could say, "I am dying beyond my means..." as Oscar Wilde said to set others at ease about his impending death! As they reach out to others, they can sometimes find themselves involved in too many places and with too many people at once, making them feel scattered and *unfocused*. They may need to focus their attention on what really matters most to them and learn to spend their energy and time where it counts.

IMPASSIONED........can become Excitable

When they believe in something, they really believe! They will be so inspired that they are *impassioned* to share their feelings and stories with others. The last restaurant they went to was simply the best place they have ever eaten, so you must go there! The last movie they saw was the best movie, so you have to see it! Sometimes they can seem so *excitable* that people won't trust anything that the high *I*s say to be real or attainable. *I*s can share how they feel, but they need to learn to be a little more realistic and careful not to exaggerate in their storytelling.

INVOLVED.........can become Directionless

The high *I* loves to be in the middle of whatever everyone else is doing. *I*s put their heart and soul into what they are doing at the moment, so watch out! Learning to choose with whom they become *involved* is an important step for the *I* type. When the winds of adversity blow or popular opinion changes, they will change, too. They may become *directionless* in their activities, because they want to experience everything!

IMAGINATIVE...can become a Daydreamer

What stories and ideas this *I* type can create! Their *imagination* can conceive what most of us would not dare to dream. Such dreams help us all to imagine a better life than we ever thought possible. And remember, a dream precedes any reality that we create. They are always wishing for or letting their minds wander off to exciting adventures. They just *know* the "biggest event" of their life is around the next corner. When out of control, their imagination can replace reality, and *daydreaming* takes over with ideas that have no foundation or purpose in achieving their dreams.

WARM and FRIENDLY..can become Purposeless

When people meet an *I*nspiring type, they feel that the high *I* is their friend because of the *warm and friendly* feelings they experience with the *I*. This is the beginning of a wonderful relationship, and the new acquaintance usually responds with warmth and friendship. Unfortunately, the high *I* can get caught up in his own feelings and be superficially friendly. The high *I* can forget about the other person's feelings as he moves on to another exciting interaction. An *I*'s initial friendly, warm interaction can quickly feel *purposeless* in forming a lasting friendship unless it is supported by genuine appreciation and interest in the other person.

This is why we give this secret tip to our *I*nspiring friends:

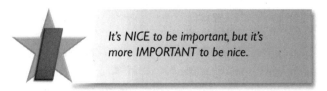

It's NICE to be important, but it's more IMPORTANT to be nice.

Attitudes and Preferences of the Inspiring Type

The star represents the *star quality* of this style! They are *I*mpressive and attractive, inspiring us to dream of a better tomorrow. We can admire their trusting and interactive style when they reach out and touch our hearts. *I*s are expressive, wanting us to feel just how they feel and to laugh with them.

The *I*nspiring type would say,

"I can't wait to have fun with you! I just know that we will have a great time together, but please hurry up! I really don't want to have to wait long. I'm not sure just what we are going to do, but don't you just love surprises? I do! Anyway, things turn out so much better if you just let them happen and keep things unstructured. What? We need to work today? Sure, we can do that. I would never want anyone at the office to be upset with me. I'll make it fun for us. Could we talk about what we're going to do? I just need to let you know how I feel. I get bored easily when I have to do something over and over or when there are too many details to keep straight. I do my best work when I'm in the mood, so I like to keep my schedule kind of flexible. We can get started soon. I wouldn't want to disappoint you! Just a minute! Well, hello! Your name is John? I'm so glad to meet you... my friend and I were just talking about..."

People You Know from the Inspiring Type

Research indicates that about 25-30 % of the general population has this *I*nspiring type profile. This **DISC** group is full of those star quality people in our world. Think of all the comedians, actors, public speakers, and entertainers in our midst. As you have read this chapter, you, no doubt, have thought of friends and relatives with this style.

There is a natural correlation between a job or role and the person who fills it. As you can imagine, *I*nspiring types become excellent actors, politicians, radio announcers, motivational speakers and auctioneers. They also make good con artists! They excel in any vocation that involves talking as the main focus.

In An Inspiring Style...

*"Death is nature's way of saying,
'Your table's ready.'"*

— Robin WIlliams

*"My most brilliant achievement was
my ability to be able
to persuade my wife to marry me."*

— Winston Churchill

*"I think I did pretty well,
considering I started out with nothing
but a bunch of blank paper."*

— Steve Martin

"You can have it all.
You just can't have it all at one time."
– Oprah Winfrey

"The very first law in advertising is
to avoid the concrete promise
and cultivate the delightfully vague."
– Bill Cosby

"Sometimes
something worth doing
is worth overdoing."
– David Letterman

"The only thing chicken about Israel —
is their soup."
– Bob Hope

"We are not retreating —
we are advancing in another direction."
– Douglas MacArthur

"Hi, I'm Robert Rohm. How do you like me so far? Well…
enough talking about me.
Let's talk about you. How do you like me?"
- Dr. Robert A. Rohm

The Inspiring Type in Review

As we have defined and described the high *I* type, you may have found many descriptions that fit you. If so, we would say that you have a high *I* personality style. On the other hand, you may feel that this chapter describes someone very different from you. In that case, we would say that you have a low *I* personality style. For an individual assessment of your personality style, the *Adult Profile Assessment* enables you to explore how the *I*nspiring type is part of your personality style. (Call our office, or visit our web site to place an order.)

We are attracted to the *I*nspiring type, because they are magnetic leaders who make life grand. They love to persuade others to their way of thinking, because they want to be popular with everyone. We can admire their ability to brighten almost any situation. This ability often earns them our recognition and approval. They want to make everything friendly and fun. For this type, life is six Saturdays in a week! They always find exciting ways to make work into play. They live by the words of comic Joe E. Lewis: "You only live once — but if you work it right, once is enough!"

We all need people with the *I*nspiring style in our lives!

Chapter Four

Introducing
the Supportive Type

The **S**upportive, high **S** type likes a calm, easygoing environment, where people are comfortable, and there are no disappointments or surprises. **S**s identify with the color blue...the most peaceful of all colors... and the color that goes well in any environment. They are reliable and **S**table, so they make it easy to live and work with them. They are satisfied with a predictable routine where things pretty much remain the same. They like to help others, so they can adapt themselves if it will help a friend. They need time to get comfortable with a new idea, but they are highly adaptable when given the time they need to process a change in their minds and get comfortable with it.

They prefer routine activities and doing one thing at a time. Routine may be boring to some people but not to them. It gives them a great deal of security knowing things are just where they should be, ready to fill someone's need. They seek to fit in and meet the needs of their family or group. They have a strong desire to serve individuals who are part of their lives. Perhaps more than any other type, the high **S** likes a **S**upportive role away from the spotlight. They are amiable and kind and would hate to upset anyone. They do not like conflict. It closes them down emotionally. This reserved and people-oriented type is a faithful and enduring friend. Unless **S**s feel secure, they may hesitate to express how they truly feel, but they will willingly listen to the feelings of another. They desire harmony and will avoid confrontation at all costs. They really appreciate your affirmation of their work and love to hear that they were helpful to you. They will maintain their relaxed and cooperative attitude while they are being steady and persistent in completing what needs to be done.

High **S**s like to maintain the **S**tatus quo, so they struggle with starting a new project. However, their **S**teady and patient nature makes them great finishers. They will work at their own pace. Like the tortoise in the fable, they will keep going until they finish whatever they start.

These individuals both communicate and desire a great deal of security. They communicate security to a friend because they want their friend to know they will always be there for them. They are loyal friends who stick by you as surely in a time of need as in your greatest hour. They can keep secrets without ever telling anyone. They desire security in their relationships, and they want to know you are always there for them. They like to be predictable, and they want to feel that they can depend on you as well.

S types are sweet. What is there not to like about a Supportive type person? They are just special. They are not pushy or bossy. You just like being around them. You feel right at home. You are very comfortable when you are with them. They always take a back seat and give others the opportunity to be first in line. Everyone responds positively to them and likes them. Ss don't do anything deliberately in order to make you like them. That's just the way they are. They would be that way even if no one else was around. High Ss are naturally passive and rather Shy. When they come into a room with a large group of people, they usually prefer to sit in the back of the room so no one will notice them. They rarely speak up in a group, unless they are called on, or someone else needs something. They enjoy watching their friends and prefer to go unnoticed, especially if they don't know the people around them. It is not that they don't like people — far from it. They love people. They are just Shy. They love to have fun, and they enjoy watching the excitement, as long as it doesn't center on them. They are naturally Supportive and have an amiable presence that makes them say,

"All for one and one for all! If we all work together, we make a great team. All of us is better than one of us!"

Strengths of the Supportive Type

All four **DISC** types have wonderful qualities that bring so much richness and diversity to our world. While we recognize that each of us has a natural personality perspective, we also recognize that we all make daily choices about the way in which we will behave. We can become aware that it is most often our strengths pushed to an extreme that cause us the most conflict in life. This next section can help the **S**upportive person to recognize the strengths of their behavior under control and see how struggles occur as those strengths are pushed out of control.

RELAXED......can become Lacking Initiative

Their *relaxed* and easygoing style will bring stability and comfort to those around them. They don't like to be pushed and can be indecisive when you ask them for an opinion. They may give two or three answers, because they don't want to create disharmony. They try to give the answer that they think you want to hear. When you ask, "What would you like to do tonight?", they will probably respond, "It doesn't matter — whatever you want to do is fine with me." In their hesitation, they can be *lacking initiative* and let opportunities pass by them. They need to learn that they are very special, and we will enjoy them more if they have the confidence to openly share their own perspective or ideas.

RELIABLE............can become Dependent

You can count on your *reliable* **S**upportive friends, because your needs are very important to them. They are practical and do what has worked in the past, so you will have no unexpected results from them. Because they need affirmation and have difficulty with the unpredictability of change, they may become *dependent* on someone else to pave the way for them in a new situation. They stand back and wait. They would rather do nothing, even if it causes them to fail. They seem to give up before they start; however, if they feel that you need them, they will do whatever you need. It is important for the high **S** to learn the value of risk and the reward of being a self-starter. After all, nothing ventured, nothing gained!

COOPERATIVE...........can become A Sucker

High **S**s are willing and able to work with people and to do what they can for others. They feel the truth of Arthur Ashe's statement, "It is not the urge to surpass others at whatever cost, but to serve others at whatever cost." When high **S**s care for you, they are very *cooperative* to come to your aid anywhere you need their help. Too often, in order to help you, they may sacrifice their own needs and become *a sucker* and let others take advantage of their good nature. Because they think of others first and cannot imagine that someone could be imposing on them, they must learn to recognize the difference between being helpful to a friend and enabling another's irresponsibility.

STABLE.................can become Indecisive

High **S**s bring stability to their family or organization, because they appreciate the success of a proven routine. They are comfortable with things that stay the same and will remind the other types to think again before making a change. It is not so much that they must have their own way. They are just trying to protect their own interests and *stability*. The other personality types know how to look out for themselves, while **S** types tend to help others to their own detriment. They will use a very low-key approach, making sure others cannot detect that they are actually protecting their own interests. If they feel that they are being pressured to move too quickly, they may become *indecisive* and then stubborn, holding on to what is familiar to them. When they begin to respect their own needs like they respect the needs of others, they can get under control and maintain their stability.

GOOD LISTENER...can become Uncommunicative

Everyone appreciates what a *good listener* the high **S** is! High **S**s will spend many hours listening to how someone else feels, because they truly do care. Even while they listen to our feelings and needs, they can be *uncommunicative* about how they feel. They think that their situations are not as bad as others, so there is no need to talk about themselves. They can be left carrying their own burdens and the burdens of the rest of the world. They can learn that part of being a good listener is not only offering sympathy, but offering encouragement to you to do something positive about the situation. Perhaps Mother Teresa of Calcutta shared this secret for the high **S** when she said, "Kind words can be short and easy to speak, but their echoes are truly endless."

SINGLE-MINDED..............can become Inflexible

Once a process or system has been put in place, they will be very true and faithful to the system. Other ideas or methods may be presented, but they will reject them, preferring instead to stay with what they know will work. They reject the idea that, "You never know until you try." They will *single-mindedly* focus on completing a process. They can become *inflexible* about trying new ideas or ways of doing things that could really benefit them, especially if they are confronted or surprised. They need time to finish what they have started, and then they can be more cooperative.

STEADFAST.....can become Resistant to Change

You may be ready to skip to the next chapter of this book, but the *steadfast* **S** has just gotten comfortable at this point and will appreciate the upcoming insights that you may miss! They will be firm in using tried and proven methods in everything they do. Even though times will change, they tend to be *resistant to the change* that must first occur for their own personal or professional growth. Even though it is uncomfortable for them, they can learn to accept changes, and when they do, they will make the change useful and helpful to everyone!

SOFTHEARTED...can become Easily Manipulated

In a coldhearted world, the *softhearted* high **S** will bring a tenderness and care that others really appreciate. The **S** type is also sentimental. **S**s know what they like, and they like what is old and familiar. They have favorite movies, memories and moods. When a special occasion arises, they spend time treasuring the memories of the past and talking about the good times that they shared. It bothers them when places from their childhood change. They like things to remain as they always have been. They save their old yearbooks, love notes, poems and many keepsakes. Unfortunately, through their sentimental nature and kindness, they can be *easily manipulated* to serve the selfish intentions of others. They can easily feel sorry for someone and feel that they have to help. The **S**upportive type can learn to choose not to rescue someone else. They will find that someimes the other person will be better off to feel the effects of his or her mistakes, so the person will be motivated to learn from those mistakes. This may feel harsh to the high **S**, but this kind of lesson can often save someone from other more painful mistakes.

SYSTEMATIC.............can become Too Slow

The high **S** will do paperwork and repetitive tasks the same way over and over again. **S**s would agree with Abraham Lincoln when he said, "Nothing valuable can be lost by taking time." While being *systematic* ensures that they will get predictable results, others can be frustrated when **S**s are so concerned about following the system that they are *too slow* in getting things done. Sometimes speed is important, too, and the **S**upportive type can learn to appreciate this truth. They may need to learn to ask for help themselves!

AMIABLE...............can become Resentful

The **S**upportive type will receive you with a gentle smile and an *amiable* greeting. Mother Teresa spoke for high **S**s when she said, "Let us make one point, that we meet each other with a smile,

46

when it is difficult to smile. Smile at each other, make time for each other in your family." High **S**s can easily come alongside you and seem satisfied just to be with you. If someone needs their help, they will happily help that person. Sometimes **S**s offer help when they really should not, either because the other person is taking advantage of them and doesn't really appreciate what they are doing, or because they are ignoring their own essential needs. Even if they continue to help, they may inwardly become *resentful* and hold a grudge against the other person. A grudge kills a relationship that might have continued to grow.

Supportive **S**s should remember their Secret Tip:

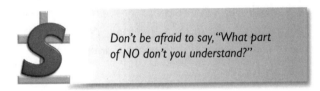

Don't be afraid to say, "What part of NO don't you understand?"

Attitudes and Preferences of the Supportive Type

The plus or minus sign represents the adaptability of this style! They adapt, because they feel that whatever you want is more or less all right with them. They are gentle and **S**upportive and want to do whatever they can to meet the needs of their family and friends. We can admire their servant's heart and their cooperative style. **S**s are amiable. They want to be sure that everyone feels comfortable and relaxed.

The **S**upportive type might say,

"Teamwork and cooperation are important for all of us. When we work together, everyone does a better job. I like to stick with what I know is best, and I would feel comfortable helping you with some of those repetitive tasks that no one else wants to do. I really don't mind. If we can find a process to use, we can feel secure in our work. A daily

routine seems to work best, so we know what to expect. We can do one thing at a time, and we can help each other. Would that be all right with you? How would you like to do it? This might be a good plan, because it is easier for everyone and eliminates some risks and problems. We all work better together if we can avoid conflict, which I have to admit makes me really uncomfortable. And please don't be surprised if I am rather quiet when we are in a large group. I enjoy being with you, but I would prefer to let you speak for us when there are lots of people listening. I can adjust to the needs of our group and help to keep harmony, so just let me know what you want me to do. If we have to work out complex problems, we may need to help each other and do it together. We may even find someone else to help with any critical analysis. Would that be okay with you?"

People You Know from the Supportive Type

Research indicates that about 30 to 35% of the general population has this **S**upportive type profile. This is the largest **DISC** group. We appreciate these kind and **S**teady people in our lives. As you have read this chapter, you, no doubt, have thought of friends and relatives with this style.

There is a natural correlation between a job or role and the person who fills it. As you can imagine, **S**upportive types become excellent diplomats, teachers, nurses, human resource directors, counselors and advisors. They develop into able vice presidents! They fill a **S**upportive role with their team. **S**s often do work outside their role description, so that the other members of the team can do their best work.

In A Supportive Style...

"Everybody today seems to be in such a terrible rush, anxious for greater developments and greater riches and so on, so that children have very little time for their parents. Parents have very little time for each other; and in the home begins the disruption of the peace of the world."

— Mother Teresa of Calcutta

"The best thing about the future is that it comes only one day at a time."

— Abraham Lincoln

"We will have to repent in this generation not merely for the hateful words and actions of the bad people but for the appalling silence of the good people."

— Martin Luther King, Jr.

"Cherish your human connections: your relationships with friends and family."

— Barbara Bush

"You can do what you have to do, and sometimes you can do it even better than you think you can."

— Jimmy Carter

"I'm going to marry a Jewish woman, because I like the idea of getting up Sunday morning and going to the deli."

— Michael J. Fox

- *"First you say that one*
over there is right.
Then you say the one over there is right.
They can't both be right."

- *"You know something my friend...*
you are right, too!"

-Tevya, Fiddler on the Roof

The Supportive Type in Review

As we have defined and described the high **S** type, you may have found many descriptions that fit you. If so, we would say that you have a high **S** personality style. On the other hand, you may feel that this chapter describes someone very different from you. In that case, we would say that you have a low **S** personality style. For an individual assessment of your personality style, the *Adult Profile Assessment* enables you to explore how the **S**upportive type is part of your personality style. (Call our office, or visit our web site to place an order.)

We are attracted to the **S**upportive type, because **S**s are servant leaders who *walk* with us. Patient and persistent, they gently advise and guide, while they do what they can to make life run more smoothly for all of us. They are faithful to serve, and they help others to be more tolerant of one another by the example of their steady and loyal style. They are often the calm in the midst of a storm, offering a peaceful and rational response in a crisis. This response restores an environment that is comfortable for high **S**s — one that is harmonious, predictable and **S**table. Although they may never tell you directly, they need your appreciation for their help and your affirmation of their special place in your heart. Their basic priority is predictability. They keep a steady pace and seek to provide security for their family first. High **S**s, when under control, are caregivers and teachers who stand with us through difficulty, helping us learn and grow to be all that we can be.

We all need people with the **S**upportive style in our lives!

Chapter Five

Introducing
the Cautious Type

Whoever said, "Measure twice... and cut once!" must have been a Cautious high C type! Carefully exploring all options and studying all related information is extremely valuable to the high C type. Cs will validate the quality of information and then develop a procedure using their data that will help them prevent making mistakes. They identify with the color yellow because, like the yellow traffic light, Caution describes their approach in all they do. Yellow also makes us think of the *radiant energy* of the sun, and Cautious types seem to radiate that kind of intensity.

High Cs are Calculating and inquisitive as they investigate, categorize and organize information. The high C type is often thought of as being "compartmental" because high Cs like to take everything and put them in boxes. Then they put the boxes in rows! Everything has a place, and everything should be in its place for the Cautious type. Cs need to understand their own proper place. They want to know how they fit in any situation. They are concerned with using proper etiquette, so they are polite with others and expect others to be polite to them in return. They want to play by the rules, and they expect everyone else to play by the rules, as well.

Abraham Lincoln once said, "Tact is the ability to describe others as they see themselves." This defines tact for the reserved and task-oriented high Cs, who are naturally diplomatic. They can separate themselves from their own feelings and recognize the perspective of another person. Their tactful and reserved nature sometimes keeps them from sharing their true feelings. They tend to focus, instead, on the facts pertinent to a situation. Because of their analytical approach, they can often recognize underlying truths about people and situations. However, they may not be aware of their own feelings about the same people and situations. Perhaps more than any other type, high **C**s have difficulty acknowledging their own feelings and being aware of the intensity of those feelings. When they ignore their feelings for too long, they can become moody or temperamental as the full force of their feelings hits them in the face. They finally must respond to their emotions!

Careful attention to details and rigorous adherence to rules make high **C**s **C**onscientious and meticulous in the detailed work they enjoy. They love flow charts, orderliness and organization. Because they highly value analyzing the facts about anything, they are thorough in their evaluation, and they will hesitate to decide anything quickly. I jokingly say that they proofread Xerox copies! Needing information validated by expert opinion, they have great difficulty with intuitive decisions that must be made without sufficient facts. This means that high **C**s will give a good objective analysis of a situation. However, because they are not people-oriented, that analysis usually will not make allowances for the feelings of the people involved in that situation. They think that people should act upon facts, not on their own irrational feelings.

Other personality types may talk things out but not the high **C**. The **C**autious type is **C**ontemplative, thinking things through before taking any action. They *know* that they *know* what they *know*! They do their homework. They research, gather facts, develop a plan of action and follow it. They do not offer their opinion about any subject until their viewpoint is well developed. They would teach, "Plan your work… then work your plan!" This is a secret to understanding the **C**ompetent high **C**.

A theoretical thinker, the high **C** loves to question and validate information. The **C**ognitive skills of **C**s allow them to see a better idea, and they will go to any length to achieve excellence. Expect a **C**autious type to be accurate and exacting, seeking precise answers and expecting quality information. Giving an estimate, using round numbers and going on your gut feelings or instincts are all examples of shoddy work to them! They are blessed and cursed with being perfectionistic in their expectations. They simply expect that doing your best is assumed, and your best should be as perfect as you can make it *and* a little better. This is why the **C**autious type says,

> "Anything worth doing is worth doing correctly. One must provide quality goods and services through careful and conscientious work."

The Strengths of the Cautious Type

All four **DISC** types have wonderful qualities that bring so much richness and diversity to our world. While we recognize that each of us has a natural personality perspective, we also recognize that each of us makes choices each day about the way in which we will behave. We can become aware that it is most often our strengths pushed to an extreme that cause us the most difficulty in life. This next section can help the **C**autious **C**s to recognize the strengths of their behavior under control and see how struggles occur as those strengths are pushed out of control.

Orderly.................can become Compulsive

In the children's book *Alice's Adventures in Wonderland*, the King explains to Alice how to be *orderly* just like our high **C** friends:

> "Where shall I begin, please, your Majesty?" she asked.
>
> "Begin at the beginning," the King said gravely, "and go on till you come to the end: then stop."

It's as simple as that to the high **C**! **C**s are businesslike and orderly. They focus on the task at hand. They can stay on track with a project long after others have given up. They enjoy putting together jigsaw or crossword puzzles, because they love to see things fall into place step by step. They have little time for nonsense. Most of life is serious to them. Just like on the fifties television police show, *Dragnet*, they want what Sergeant Friday would request:

> "Just the facts, ma'am — just the facts!"

As their intense focus increases, they can become so concerned about every detail that they become *compulsive* about little issues which are not important. This frustrates people who work with them and may cause people to give up trying to satisfy the high expectations of the high Cs. Cautious Cs must learn the difference between seeking excellence and expecting perfection, both in themselves and others with whom they work.

LOGICAL......................can become Critical

The high **C** must make *logical* sense of everything. Cs tend to ignore their feelings in favor of logical facts. They will carefully and completely think through every part of a procedure and every piece of data gathered. In their never ending quest for perfection, others may feel that they are just *critical* of everything and everybody. When they are out of control, their critical nature may drive people away from them. Perhaps they can learn from Michael J. Fox, who said, "I am careful not to confuse excellence with perfection. Excellence, I can reach for; perfection is God's business."

INTENSE.................can become Unsociable

When they are focused, nothing can pull them away. The world can totally pass by them, and they see only what is within their focus. I once knew a high **C** , whose family joked with her by saying, "The house could burn down around you, and you would still be sitting on that couch reading your book!" She admitted that this was probably true! With this kind of *intensity*, they can become *unsociable,* concentrating on their task to the exclusion of other people. Michelangelo was a gifted high **C** artist who said, "While you are alone, you are entirely your own master, and if you have one companion, you are but half your own and the less so in proportion to the indiscretion of his behavior." Does that sound a bit unsociable? And yet his intensity created the magnificent paintings of the Sistine Chapel that we still treasure today, some five hundred years later. We hope that Michelangelo also took time to be social and relax with his friends!

CURIOUS.....................can become Nosey

The high **C** is insatiably *curious*. **C**s just seem to be interested in knowing more about everything. They usually have just one more question that needs to be answered before any conclusion can be drawn. They collect facts about people, too. This desire for the facts causes them to be *nosey* about the personal lives of others. High **C**s may ignore their own feelings, but if they want to enjoy friendships with other people, they need to learn to respect the feelings of others.

TEACHABLE.....can become Easily Offended

Their quest for knowledge and quality answers makes **C**s very *teachable*. They always want to learn about new technology, and they are interested in the development of procedures in their business. They want to understand and be included in what others are doing. They love to discuss theories and concepts. If someone's approach takes issue with the correctness of the way they have already been doing something, they can become *easily offended* and defensive against all suggestions. Because they are thorough and **C**autious, they hate to be told that they are wrong. They need to be convinced that their old way was right, but the new way is better.

CAUTIOUS.....................can become Fearful

High **C**s are *cautious* about considering a risk. They never want to make a mistake. **C** types are loyal to ideas and principles. When **C**autious types find themselves in unknown territory, they feel uncertain and threatened. Their loyalty is first to the ideas or principles and then to the people involved in a situation. We might say that they are loyal as long as they know all the details of the plan. But when details unravel, their loyalty unravels. They are constantly checking themselves and may become so *fearful* of breaking the rules or doing something wrong, that they can become immobilized into inactivity. We can appreciate their **C**autious ability to predict and prevent many costly mistakes. We can also encourage them to recognize why the risk of doing something wrong is often less important than the failure that may result from doing nothing.

CORRECT......................can become Rigid

The high **C** would say, "Do it right, or don't do it at all!" **C**s want to be *correct*, so they will carefully follow rules and procedures. **C**s are very consistent. You can set your watch by them. You can usually depend on what they tell you, because they have already verified their information before sharing it with you. They are rarely incorrect in the details of a story. When they are convinced they are right about a detail or a concept, there is no changing their mind. Their intense need to follow protocol, and their comprehensive evaluation of information, can cause them to be too *rigid*. They may permit no allowance for human emotions or limitations. You may think you can persuade them differently about their conclusion, but once they have evaluated all the facts, that is usually not the case. Remember this proverb: "He who is convinced against his will is of the same opinion still." This really applies to a **C**. While it is difficult for a high **C** to acknowledge, we can all remember that sometimes maintaining an ongoing relationship is more important than proving we are right.

QUESTIONING.........can become Doubtful

The high **C** is always *questioning*. **C**s ask the questions that must be asked and the ones that others have missed. **C**s are so idealistic. They want to be the best, look for the best and produce the best. They like things to fit together in a nice, neat package. They hate having loose ends or unfinished business in their lives. **C**s don't like things to end abruptly or unexpectedly. They try to bring closure to all of their experiences and are frustrated by things in life that cannot be explained. If an issue depends heavily upon emotion or really has no clear, indisputable answer, they may become *doubtful* of everything and everybody and lose their focus. They need to find a view of their world that is bigger than they are, and in that view, establish truth for themselves.

CONSCIENTIOUS.....can become Worrisome

High **C**s will *conscientiously* cover every detail of their work. **C** types are self-sacrificing and committed to producing quality work. They have the enviable ability to stick with the task at hand and will work tirelessly to do a good job. They constantly look for ways to make a situation better. They desire excellence and strive for perfection, even when it means long, hard hours. Every piece of paperwork will be completed, copied and filed. As their role and responsibilities expand, they will have a tendency to be *worrisome* over all the details that must be handled correctly. Perhaps they can learn from this wise saying:

> *Remember that fear always lurks behind perfectionism. Confronting your fears and allowing yourself to be human can, paradoxically, make you a far happier and more productive person.*

PRECISE.......................can become Picky

All the numbers and *precise* facts given to you by high **C**s will usually be correct. You can be sure that they are right about their facts. They recognize the importance of a factual analysis of a situation. Sometimes the exacting particulars of a situation are of less consequence than the feelings of the people involved or the relationship those people enjoy. **C**s keep a tight rein on their emotions, and they expect others to do the same. They can be *picky* about individual elements and the manner in which they are defined and expressed, while discounting emotions and individual limitations. They may need to show others why they feel the need to be so exact, or they can be perceived as critical.

They must learn the truth of their secret tip:

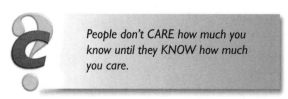

People don't CARE how much you know until they KNOW how much you care.

Attitudes and Preferences of the Cautious Type

The question mark represents the importance of fact-finding for this style! They are assessing and exacting, seeking the best quality in everything. We can admire their accuracy and inquiring mind. Cs are Conscientious - intense in their quest for truth and certainty.

The Cautious type would say,

"I like work involving critical analysis and research. I need time to validate my work. In order to do my best work, I must avoid making quick decisions, and I will also avoid unplanned or spontaneous activities. While others may enjoy surprises, I really don't like them. I would rather make plans and follow them. This eliminates many mistakes. This insight is valuable to me, because I really don't like being forced to accommodate imperfections in anything. I want my role to be clearly defined, so that I can work within the established structure. I expect a lot from myself, and I expect you to feel the same way about your work. When we work on the same project, I assume that we will produce quality results. I hope you can understand that this is very important to me, because I don't like compromising my standards for the sake of maintaining harmony. I like you; I just like you enough to expect the best from you! I really don't like confronting others, but if an issue of accuracy or quality is involved, I have to speak up. We should do things the right way and produce something truly excellent."

People You Know from the Cautious Type

Research indicates that about 20 – 25% of the general population has this Cautious type profile. This means there are more Cs than Ds but fewer of these than our people-oriented Is and Ss. We value the traits of the Cs. We recognize the quality work of high Cs that we know. As you have read this chapter, you, no doubt, have thought of friends and relatives with this style.

There is a natural correlation between a job or role and the person who fills it. As you can imagine, Cautious types become good professionals, because they do well when they develop expertise in a particular field. They are usually excellent teachers or professors, because they love to learn. Cs also make great inventors, researchers and scientists. They have the ability to do several hundred experiments without giving up their search for a solution. Thomas Edison was once asked if he was ever discouraged in his work of inventing the incandescent light bulb. (He had tried over 2,000 experiments before beginning to make real progress.) He replied, "Not at all, for I knew for sure 2,000 ways it would not work!" What a great Cautious style statement!

Cs make excellent musicians. Music allows high Cs to express their feelings and their aesthetic sensitivity within a structure of rules. They have the self-discipline required to practice daily and get the notes exactly right. They also make good artists in a variety of different fields of work. They have an intense desire to create something that will improve our quality of life. They want to make their world a better place. After all…they have a better idea!

Cs make good philosophers. They seek long-term solutions rather than easy answers. They want to understand why our world works as it does. Their analytical nature gives their theoretical minds the reasoning power they need to fit ideas together and then to take them apart again.

In A Cautious Style...

"Skeptical scrutiny is the means,
in both science and religion,
by which deep insight
can be winnowed from deep nonsense."

– Dr. Carl Sagan, astronomer

"Frankly Captain,
that doesn't seem logical."

– Spock, from Star Trek

"People must not do things for fun.
We are not here for fun. There is no
reference to fun in any Act of Parliament."

– A.P. Herbert, British author and
politician, 1890-1971

"Often you have to rely on intuition."

– Bill Gates

"If we do what is necessary,
all the odds are in our favor."

– Henry Kissinger

"Let the wise listen and add to their learning,

and let the discerning get guidance."

– Solomon – Proverbs 1:5

"You cannot hope to build a better world without improving the individuals. To that end, each of us must work for our own improvement and, at the same time, share a general responsibility for all humanity, our particular duty being to aid those to whom we think we can be most useful."

— *Madame Marie Curie*

"It's all happening too fast.
I've got to put the brakes on,
or I'll smack into something."

— *Mel Gibson*

"They that will not be counseled,
cannot be helped. If you do not hear reason
she will rap you on the knuckles."
— *Benjamin Franklin*

"Just because something doesn't
do what you planned it to do,
doesn't mean it's useless."
— *Thomas Edison*

"There is a big difference between good sound
reasoning...and reasoning that sounds good."

— *Dr. Norman Geisler*

The Cautious Type in Review

As we have defined and described the high **C** type, you may have found many descriptions that fit you. If so, we would say that you have a high **C** personality style. On the other hand, you may feel that this chapter describes someone very different from you. In that case, we would say that you have a low **C** personality style. For an individual assessment of your personality style, the *Adult Profile Assessment* enables you to explore how the **C**autious type is part of your personality style. (Call our office, or visit our web site to place an order.)

We are attracted to the **C**autious type, because they are **C**onscientious leaders who lead from foundational principles, and they expect the best from each individual. **C**areful and **C**ontemplative, they see pitfalls that other styles may miss. **C**s seek an environment with structure in order to maintain the highest standards and productivity. Their intense desire for perfection lights the way to the quality answers, value and excellence they need. They shine brightest in a profession or specialty that takes advantage of their accuracy and thorough competency. Their underlying priority is correct procedure, working within a framework that will establish new levels of excellence. High **C**s, when under control, are theoretical and exacting. They are able to carve out the bedrock of philosophy and facts, and they will build on this foundation to reach new heights of creative excellence.

We all need people with the **C**autious style in our lives!

Chapter Six

What's Your PQ?

Your Personality Quotient

At an early age, we remember being in school and hearing about something called **IQ**. We did not know what it meant, but we knew that it was important. Parents, as well as teachers, put a lot of emphasis on your IQ. Some people were even placed in certain groups at school based on their IQ.

As children, we did not know how you got an IQ, nor what to do to make it better, but we became aware that "being smart" played a very important role in your school life. As adults, these things make more sense. Your IQ is important. We now understand that IQ, your *Intelligence Quotient*, measures how quickly we learn but not how much we can learn. We also know that a high IQ alone does not guarantee success in life or in relationships.

Several excellent articles and books have been written about other key ingredients to success in life. Have you heard about **EQ**? This is your *Emotional Quotient*. It is your ability to recognize how you and those around you are feeling, as well as the ability to generate, understand and regulate emotions. Scientific research shows that different parts of the brain have different purposes, and that emotional responses come from specific areas of the brain. The information is all quite technical, and it shows that emotional intelligence is separate from other kinds of intelligence. We commonly call it intuition, instinct or a *gut feeling*. EQ is the basis for judgment when we choose something based upon the feeling that we like it and think that it just feels right. As you can well imagine, your EQ can be related to your personality style, because it shows your sensitivity to your own feelings and other people's emotions. Studies

63

show that your EQ is an important factor in your success in life.

What about your *AQ*? Your Adversity Quotient measures your ability to respond effectively to adversity. This is also related to your personality style. Factors influencing your AQ are control, ownership, effect and endurance. The first factor is control. Taking control in all areas over which you have control is important. On the other hand, you may spend a great deal of emotional energy worrying about areas over which you have little, or no, control. These tendencies can be predicted through understanding your personality style.

The second factor in your Adversity Quotient is ownership. That is your ability to take responsibility for your part in the problem and its solution. Taking responsibility for your part, while leaving the responsibility of others with them, allows you to spend your energy working out a good solution for your part. If you take responsibility for the parts of the problem that really are not yours, you will probably be very frustrated by the limitations on what you can do, and you may miss taking care of your part. Simply stated, you cannot control other people, but you can control yourself.

The third factor in your AQ is limiting the effects of a crisis to appropriate areas in your life. That will keep you from making the problem bigger than it really is. This involves understanding your personality style and staying under control. Each **DISC** type has a different struggle in this area.

The last area is endurance. Your endurance needs to be stronger than the problem. Each **DISC** type has traits that help or hinder endurance. The **D** and **S** styles will usually endure - the **D**s because of their tenacious will to win and the **S**s because of their stubbornness under stress. The **I**s endure by relying on their optimism and the strength of the encouragement that others give them. The **C**s endure because they anticipated the adversity and expected to deal with it in the first place! How you deal with the adversity that we all encounter in life is vital to your success.

Becoming aware of your natural tendencies is the first step toward using them. Some of these tendencies are helpful to your success, and some of them become roadblocks preventing your success. As you understand yourself better, you empower yourself to improve!

> The most **natural** thing in all of life is to see things from your own perspective. But, the most **supernatural** thing you can learn to do is see things from the perspective of others.

May we introduce you to what we believe is, perhaps, the most important quotient in your life? Your **PQ**, or **P**ersonality **Q**uotient, is your ability to understand yourself and others for effective communication and teamwork.

We all desire the personal satisfaction coming from a feeling of security and the knowledge of our own significance in life. As you read about the **DISC** personality types, you may have begun to recognize that personal satisfaction looks different to an **I**nspiring type than it does to a **C**autious type! As your awareness of your unique perspective grows, so does your ability to make choices that are right for you. You feel more secure and, therefore, more successful as you make those good choices.

Something else also happens. You begin to be more aware of those around you. Who else did you think about as you explored the **DISC** types? Perhaps you thought of your husband or wife, your parent, child or friend. Unless you live alone on an island, you will have contact with other people — family members, fellow workers, church family, friends, neighbors and professional or business associates. As you become more aware of their personality styles, you can begin to understand them better. You can begin to see that you have a significant role in their lives, and they are important to you, as well.

This awareness of yourself, and then of others, are the first two parts of your PQ. Your success in life will depend, in many ways, on your PQ, because your self-awareness and awareness of others give you the ability to relate to others effectively. If you only understand life from your own perspective, which is the most natural way to view things, you will often fail to communicate and work effectively with others. We need to learn to see things from another personality perspective. This begins by becoming truly aware of our own behavior and natural perspective. In this way, we can begin to see that there are different sides to a story and many aspects of a situation. We can really see that there is a bigger picture than our own!

The Four Steps

We have taken these principles of awareness and understanding, and have simplified them into four steps. These steps empower you to

raise your awareness and to explore the keys to raising your **P**ersonality **Q**uotient. You will now be able to answer the question, "What's your **PQ**?"

PQ Step One

As you have read the previous chapters, you have begun to **DISC**over personality types. You have probably already begun to increase your self-awareness, relating both to how you naturally behave, and how you may choose to behave. Awareness is the first step in understanding yourself within the scope of your personality style.

As you begin to be aware of your distinct actions and your own patterns of behavior, you will understand your own personality style and that will help you see more objectively what you do. We will discuss this step in the next chapter.

PQ Step Two

Understanding another person, and how that person's personality perspective may be different from yours, is the second step. Simply becoming aware of and being able to focus on another person's perspective objectively, outside your own frame of reference, is such an enlightening experience! You may truly be able to see life through that person's eyes for the first time. We will explore this more fully in Chapter Eight.

PQ Step Three

The next step is where your awareness and understanding really create a positive effect. As you understand your own personality, and the personality of another person, you can learn to relate to him or her differently. You can learn to say and do things in ways that relate to that person from his or her perspective instead of yours! We call this adapting your style.

Taking the third step, adapting your style, empowers you to create better relationships. It enables you to adapt your words and actions toward others so that you communicate effectively with them. You will communicate with them according to their personality style, rather than your own, as you learn to speak from a perspective that is responsive to the needs and interests of others. This communication key unlocks the door to better relationships. Look forward to Chapter Nine for this third step!

PQ Step Four

As you build better relationships with those around you, you can take your awareness to a whole new level. You will begin to recognize that individual relationships sometimes become part of a bigger picture. This happens in a family, where more than two people relate to each other. It also occurs in the workplace any time that more than two people work together to do something that no one person could do as well alone. This is the fourth step, which is building better teams.

Step Four expands the scope of your effective communication to include a group of people who function as a team. This is an exceptional experience that is all too rare. In many ways, it is like the magical camp experience you may have had as a child or teenager. Did you ever have an experience like that?

You spend a week at a camp, maybe willingly, or perhaps unwillingly. You do things with your cabin mates, and you share part of yourself with them. You like one or two of your cabin mates, you dislike one and the rest are just okay. Your counselor manages to draws the group together. Then something begins to happen. You begin to enjoy being with your group and you appreciate how the group makes you feel. You seem to become the best *you* with them. When you play games, you root for your cabin mates. You eat together. You sleep in the same room. You pull pranks on one another! Wow, it's fun!

You shared an experience with a group that was very special. You may have wanted or even tried to repeat the experience and regain the feeling of that time, but it was never exactly the same. This is one way to recognize a real team. The group seems to have a synergy that grows from the people and situation involved. Somehow the group comes to life, and each person is part of what is created by the team.

How does this happen? You will not only have an individual relationship with each person on the team, but they will have individual relationships with one another, as well. These relationships will affect the team as a whole, and yet, the team has a life of its own. You begin to recognize and appreciate the strengths and struggles of each person on the team. The team begins to draw on the strengths of each personality style, and the synergy really shows that *Together Everyone Achieves More!* This is step four - Building Better, More Effective Teams. We will introduce this step in Chapter Ten.

Raise your awareness and effectiveness through your PQ... your Personality Quotient!

Four Steps to Raising Your PQ

1. Understanding yourself through your personality style
2. Understanding another person through his or her personality style
3. Adapting your style to create better relationships
4. Building better teams where ...

Together Everyone Achieves More!

Understanding Begins with Awareness

We have introduced your Personality Quotient and have discussed its importance in finding satisfaction in life. Awareness is the key that opens the door to each of these steps. Awareness begins with being alert and observing your own behavior. We can illustrate how growing awareness is like putting together a puzzle. How can you begin to put together this puzzle, to increase your awareness, and to take this first step in understanding yourself? When you put together a puzzle, you start by taking the pieces out of the box and laying them face up on a table. Why? So that you can see them! You are alert. You observe the number of pieces, their shapes and their colors.

> *You cannot **beware** of something*
> *you are not first **aware** of!*

Since you most likely have done puzzles before, you either look at the picture on the box or you do not look at it! To some people, looking at the box is the first thing they do. They want to know what the picture will look like. They are cognizant of the advantage that this information will give them. They can begin to see a pattern in the pieces. To other people, looking at the box is just cheating. They prefer to discover the pattern as they put the puzzle together. They are perhaps more conscious of the shapes of the pieces, focusing their attention on placing pieces by their shape instead of their color.

> *To be aware is to be cognizant of your behavior, and to gain firsthand knowledge of yourself. You must be conscious of what you do: this means you will focus your attention on it, even to the point of preoccupation, for a time.*

There is another stark difference in people who like puzzles. We have already observed that some look at the picture, and others do not. We can also observe that some are *sensible*. They start the frame, separate the pieces by color and work on one section at a time. Because they think about different ways to match pieces, we could say that they are more logical in their approach to solving the puzzle. Others rely more on their feelings, and are more *sensitive*. They feel their way to the spot for each piece.

Whether you are more sensible, or more sensitive, in your approach to puzzling, you start a puzzle, and you soon find that you are drawn to the puzzle and cannot stop working on it. You want to find the place for just *one* more piece. You work late into the night, moving from one area to another, hoping to complete part of the picture. When this happens, we would say that you are really *alive* to the puzzle, and the puzzle has become *alive* to you! This makes it easy to stay awake and finish the puzzle. You are alert and interested, and you are excited to see your finished picture!

> *When you are truly aware, you are alive to yourself: you are acutely sensitive to your own behavior. You may feel as if you just woke up! You see yourself in an entirely new light - in ways that you have not seen previously. You feel fully awake. You are alert to once again observe and learn, to see who you really are, and to become the best that you can be.*

As you become more self-aware, you begin to put together the pieces of behavior traits in the puzzle of your personality. You see your own behavior, not to judge it, but first to simply observe it. This helps you to begin to understand more about yourself.

Let's see how you can **DISC**over more about YOU as you heighten your awareness and understanding in the next chapter!

Chapter Seven

Understanding Yourself

PQ Step One

Awareness Leads to Understanding

Have you ever done something that surprised you? We have all done something, at one time or another, that surprised everyone else, but sometimes we do things that surprise ourselves! Usually, you are keenly aware of the strange thing that you did. You feel surprised, because you do not understand why you did what you did!

Awareness brings your behavior to your attention. It is like examining the pieces of your personality puzzle. Becoming aware of your personality style is like looking at the picture on the puzzle box. You can begin to see the patterns in your own behavior. You can begin to understand how the puzzle fits together. This is understanding your personality style. You choose your behavior, and see its true colors and the effects of your choices. You understand, because you **DISC**over the patterns in what you did, and, hopefully, you gain some clues as to why you did it. This understanding teaches you more about yourself and empowers you to choose which behavior you will use the next time something similar happens. You will not be surprised the next time!

You already have some awareness of your personality style from reading the **DISC** chapters. Completing an *Adult Profile Assessment* can give you graphs of your **DISC** profile that will measure different aspects of your personality. Although it is not required for you to do a personality profile assessment before you are able to proceed in this book, the material will become more meaningful for you when you actually complete an assessment. Even if you have not completed an assessment, you will probably identify with one of the **DISC** types, and the corresponding statements from each of the charts on the following pages. Knowing the primary type in your style is usually easy. Knowing more about the other types in your style is a secret to understanding yourself as you become aware of less predominant traits and tendencies.

If you have completed one of these assessments, take a moment to review your graphs at this time. Look at your Basic Style, which is Graph II. You will notice a plotting point, whether high or low, for each **DISC** type in your style. *You've Got Style* means that you have a part of all four **DISC** types in your very special personality. Your unique personality style has some of all the traits from Very High to High, Average, Low or Very Low in each of the **D, I, S** and **C** types. No one is simply one style. We all have some of all four types in our own personality style to a greater or lesser degree. Remember, we call this your unique **D - I - S - C** personality *blend*.

As a child, do you remember playing with a wonderful light show that came in a tube? You looked in one end of that special tube, turning the other end as you held it up to the light. How delighted you were as you searched for that perfect combination of color. You watched in wonder as the light danced and played before your eyes! They called it a kaleidoscope, and it was fascinating.

Your "Personality Kaleidoscope" is just like that light show you saw as a child. The green (Go!) of the **D**, the red (Flashy!) of the **I**, the blue (Peaceful!) for the **S**, and the yellow (Caution!) of the **C** all shine in various shades in the light of your personality. This special kaleidoscope picture captures the colors of your personality style's blend of **DISC**. Think of your colors. Do you have a high **S** type in your personality style? This would put a large section of blue in your kaleidoscope. It would also give you a key to understanding yourself better as you explore the **S** personality type.

Looking at the **DISC** type that is highest in your style can show you many things. The questions on the next page can be used by each **DISC** type and will help you review specific areas of interest to your particular style.

> *What is your natural outlook on life?*
> *What really makes you tick?*
> *What is your focus in addressing important issues*
> *and in solving pressing problems?*
> *What environment is best for you to feel comfortable,*
> *so that you can do your best work?*

For example, I have a very high **I** type personality style. I am very outgoing and very people-oriented. I like to persuade others to my way of thinking while having fun in the process! I like an environment that is friendly, fun and exciting! On the other hand, high **D** types like to be in charge of projects while staying focused on getting things done. I have often compared them to a heat-seeking missile. As we say down south, "They know how to 'get after' something!" They like an environment that is upbeat, fast-paced and powerful. The opposite is true as well. **S**s may enjoy a nice quiet evening with a close friend watching a video they have seen over and over. **C**s may enjoy an evening alone reading a good book. How different we are!

Think carefully about your style as you read the charts that follow. Take a moment to become more aware of your tendencies. You can observe your own behavior in some of these descriptions. You may want to highlight or circle the statements that you feel apply to you.

Outlook on Life

... likes to lead or be in charge

... likes to persuade others to his or her way of thinking

...likes to provide necessary support to help complete the job

... likes consistent quality and excellence

How does your outlook on life affect what you do? It is your starting point - the perspective from which you look at any situation in life. When our Personality Insights team began to work on this book, everyone played a different role. The high **D** style gave us the challenge of creating this book. They decided what we needed to do, and who would do what. I used my high **I** style to add some good stories and illustrations that would give some *life* to the book. I also tried to inspire everyone with the potential significance of the project. The **S** style completed his tasks, kept us working as a team and made sure that everyone had coffee. The high **C** style shared quality material that would give substance to the book. The **C** style also proofread each revision.

We each approached our project from a different perspective because of our difference of outlook on life, and this difference is the strength of our team! In the same way, your outlook on life gives you a special approach to everything you do.

Focus

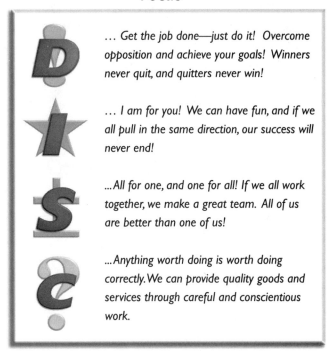

... Get the job done—just do it! Overcome opposition and achieve your goals! Winners never quit, and quitters never win!

... I am for you! We can have fun, and if we all pull in the same direction, our success will never end!

...All for one, and one for all! If we all work together, we make a great team. All of us are better than one of us!

...Anything worth doing is worth doing correctly. We can provide quality goods and services through careful and conscientious work.

Focus comes into play when we encounter problems or adversity. What do we focus on when a challenge arises? Looking at the list above, we can see what a difference this creates! Do you just push ahead or look to the group for a tension-breaking laugh? Do you look for ways that you can help someone in the group so that the project can be completed, or do you sit back and figure out the correct way to do something? One of these aspects will be your main focus as you encounter challenges. Your other types will also play a supporting role as you focus on solving your daily challenges.

For example, a person who has a style blend having a high **D** and a secondary **C** will find the correct solution so that he or she can quickly get the job done. That blend does not want to come back and fix another problem created by a hasty solution. The secondary trait serves the highest type as this individual focuses on getting the job done, while doing it correctly. By the way, this style makes a great trial attorney!

> *The way your four traits work together in your own personality style is called your* **Style Blend.**

Our environment always affects us. A certain environment may make it harder for us to concentrate or communicate, while a change of environment may make those things easier. All of us have an ideal environment, where we are most comfortable and best able to relate, communicate and accomplish our best work.

Ideal Environment

...Upbeat, fast, powerful

...Fun, friendly, exciting

...Predictable, stable, harmonious

...Structured with procedures, accuracy, quality

Your Ideal Environment is the situation that you like best. It is one in which you can relax and relate to people and feel invigorated to do your best work. For example, an ideal environment for a **C** type would have structure for procedures, accuracy and quality. Yet this would be a stressful environment for an **I** type who wants an environment that is fun, friendly and exciting! Remember how I often say that opposites attract? People who have different styles often marry, and then must live together. *Opposites attract, then they attack!* We really need to understand our differences concerning an ideal environment! Think about a time when you did your best work. You will probably find that this situation created an ideal environment for you to interact and perform.

Basic Needs

...Challenge, choices, control

...Recognition, approval, popularity

...Appreciation, security, assurance

...Quality answers, value, excellence

One of my favorite thoughts that I love to say is, *"People do not do things against you. They do things for themselves!"* That means that all of us naturally seek to meet our own basic needs. Sometimes, these needs are easily met, but often we search for additional ways to meet them. We point out in our Personality Insights training programs that people often will give their mate what they themselves need, unaware that their mate may need something very different!

Understanding our own basic needs can also help us see what may have prompted us to do something that another may misunderstand. How different is a **D** type, who needs challenge and control, from an **S** type, who needs security and appreciation!

The sad truth is that we often give people what *we* need, not what *they* need! Sometimes a person who is a high **I**, needing recognition and approval, tells a high **C** person to stand up and take a bow in front of the group. Can you see that this doesn't meet the need of the person who is a high **C**? The same thing happens when a high **C** person tries to sell a high **I** something by giving a detailed analysis of the quality of a product. The high **I** just wants to know if other people like it and if using it will be simple and fun! Giving other people what *they* need really satisfies them, which in the end, will really satisfy *us* as well. In order t o do this, we must first understand the basic needs and wants of each personality type.

In all of these ways, **DISC** personality types deal with life from a different perspective *every day*! You can begin to understand yourself better as you consider the previous statements that you chose to describe yourself.

In Summary

As you continue to read *You've Got Style*, take time to make the information yours by highlighting **DISC** insights that apply especially to you. Notice how your *Outlook on Life* shows in your approach to daily living. Begin to be aware of your *Focus* and how people respond to you in everyday situations, especially as adversity comes and problems arise. Recognize how you respond when your *Ideal Environment* allows you to communicate and interact more easily. Think about your decision-making processes, and explore what *basic needs* you meet as you make decisions.

You may have noticed that you felt you could relate to more than one of the statements in each of the previous sections. Just as you have all four types in your personality style, you also have a special *blending* of characteristics, or traits, in your style. We call this your *Style Blend*.

Your Style Blend

Our discussion of each **DISC** type in the previous chapters gave you a basic introduction to the classic **D, I, S** and **C** types. We know, for instance, that the high **D** is **D**ominant, **D**irect, **D**emanding, **D**ecisive, **D**etermined and a **D**oer. This is a classic, general picture but not a box in which to "pigeonhole" someone. *No one is purely one type.*

You can become aware and better understand what drives you, your real passion, and your natural perspective, by focusing on the highest type in your personality style. This is the **DISC** type you feel most describes you. It is shown in the Profile Assessment as the highest plotting point in your Graph II – Basic Style. We identify this type in your style by saying that you have, for example, a high **S** style or perhaps a high **C** style. You may have recognized that you have some behavior characteristics, or *traits*, from all four **DISC** types.

For example, you may feel that you are **D**irect and **I**nfluencing, yet **S**teady and **C**onscientious. This is why you can envision some of all four **DISC** colors in your "Personality Kaleidoscope." Your special *Style Blend* identifies the high type or types in your personality style according to their intensity in your style.

Most commonly, people have more than one high type in their personality style or more than one plotting point above the midline. About 80% of the population has more than one high type in their style. This means that they have more than one **DISC** type with which they identify. You may have 1, 2 or even 3 plotting points above the midline in your Basic Style Graph. This can feel confusing to you, but each of these high types can vary in strength or intensity, as well!

In general, one type is predominant. One or two other types may also be above the midline on your personality profile graphs but not quite as high as the highest type. This means that those traits are strong or "active" in you, as well. For example, my most predominant trait is the **I** style. But, my **D** style is also above the midline on my basic personality graph. This is an important distinction that helps me better understand which personality style I will probably utilize and what I will probably do when under stress.

The secondary high type in your personality style serves or helps your primary type by using those behavior traits to serve and accomplish your passion. For example, because I am a high **I** type, I will naturally try to influence other people in a very persuasive manner in order to reach my objectives. Since my secondary type is **D**, I will also drive very hard and decisively in order to reach my goals as quickly as possible. My next highest trait is the **S** type, which always causes me to take into account the feelings and considerations of others when I am pressing ahead on a project. I try to slow down enough to make sure everyone is still "singing off the same page!" And... I am painfully aware that my C trait is inadequate. Therefore, I bring in staff support to help in that *cautious* area. Your *Style Blend* uses the **D**, **I**, **S** and **C** types to show the blend of high types in your style. It is written like this: A **D/I** or **S/C** or an **I/SC**. The first letter denotes the highest type, and the

Understanding Style Blends

We can observe two different kinds of Style Blends. Looking again at our **DISC** circle, we learn that the most common Style Blends are with **DISC** types that are adjacent on the model:

Complementary Style Blends

D WITH C OR I

I WITH S OR D

S WITH C OR I

C WITH D OR S

These are Complementary Style Blends, because the behavior traits in these types seem to complement each other. They have one part of the **DISC** circle orientation in common. They are both Outgoing or Reserved, or they are both Task-oriented or People-oriented.

Less common Style Blends are with types that are across from each other on the model:

Contrasting Style Blends

D/S OR S/D

I/C OR C/I

These are Contrasting Style Blends, because the behavior traits in these types often seem opposite. The two types in these Style Blends are opposite for Outgoing or Reserved, and they are also opposite for Task-oriented or People-oriented. People with Contrasting Style Blends may feel that people misunderstand them, for they can behave in seemingly conflicting ways. These people may also feel more conflicted in decision-making, for they have two contrasting perspectives to balance within their own personality style. I have come to understand that these contrasting styles are, in reality, very dynamic. Just like dynamite! They can either blow you up, or they can create beautiful fireworks! Knowing how to use and control the power of your personality is the secret.

PERCENTAGES OF BLENDS IN GENERAL POPULATION

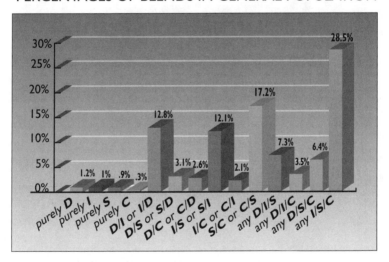

This chart shows how common your Style Blend is in the general population. For a more complete discussion of your special style blend, please refer to the *Adult Profile Assessment*. (Call our office, or visit our web site to place an order.)

After reading this material, you may, for the first time, really *feel* the differences in your personality styles when you must make a decision involving other people! This next section shares the priorities we tend to choose as we consider how to make a decision.

Making decisions

Each personality style naturally approaches decisions differently. You know some people who are very impulsive in decision-making. You know others who feel stressed if they must make any decision quickly. Understanding your decision-making style can help you become more successful in balancing the issues involved and interacting with the people who are affected by your decisions.

A Priority for Power

This Basic Priority picture shows that the higher from the midline that the **D** plotting point lies, the greater the intensity of the high **D** type in the person's style. The higher the intensity of the high **D** type, the more comfortable the person is in using **Power** to

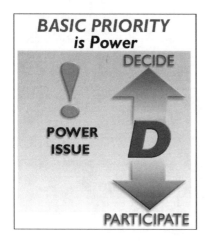

decide in order to solve problems. High **D**s lack self-doubt. They prefer to be in control. If given the option, they will happily decide for themselves and everyone else!

The lower the intensity in the **D** priority, the less comfortable a person tends to be in making quick decisions. Low **D**s prefer to use **Power** as a way for everyone to *participate* in reaching a decision with a consensus of opinion from everyone involved. They prefer to be a team player. If given the option, they will participate in the process, but in the end, they will participate by allowing the group to decide.

Do you place a lot of importance on the power of the people involved in a situation, or do you first assess your own power to solve a problem? These are the two factors in the **D** Basic Priority for Power. If **D** is the highest type in your Style Blend, you will probably find that your power to decide is most important in any decision you make. If, on the other hand, you have a very low **D** type in your style, you will be more prone to participate with others by asking the opinion of several people, and let the group make the real decision. What a difference this can make!

A good example of this difference in priorities happened in our office in Atlanta, Georgia. Ken Voges, a **C/S** Consultant from Houston, Texas, who works with Personality Insights, was deciding when to return to our office for meetings. Because he has a low **D** style, he wanted everyone to participate in this decision. He individually asked each person involved if a certain date would be acceptable to him or her. After a consensus was reached, he announced, at the staff meeting, the date of his expected meetings. One of our high **D** staff members noticed what he did and observed that she would have made the decision differently. She would have chosen a date, announced it at the staff meeting and told the group to get back to her later if the date would not work for them. Do you see that there really are *different* ways to approach a decision? Our personality types play a powerful role in all we do or say.

A Priority for People

This Basic Priority picture shows that the higher from the midline that the **I** plotting point lies, the greater the intensity of the high **I** type in the person's style. The higher the intensity of the high **I** type, the more comfortable the person is in approaching **People** to *interact* in order to persuade others. **I**s make impulsive decisions based on the approval of others. They

prefer to think out loud, and, if given the option, they will make the popular decision!

The lower the intensity of the *I* priority, the less comfortable a person is in making impulsive decisions. Low *I*s prefer to approach **People** to listen to what they say. They reach a decision logically, after listening to many viewpoints. They prefer to be persuaded. If given the option, they will *isolate* themselves and decide logically based on many facts and opinions.

Do you place more importance in your decisions on the feelings of people around you or on the logic of the different opinions offered? These are the two factors in the *I* Basic Priority for People. If *I* is the highest type in your Style Blend, you will probably find that persuading those around you is most important in any decision you make. If, on the other hand, you have a very low *I* type in your style, you will be more prone to listen to opposing arguments and logically evaluate them to reach your decision. What a difference this can make!

A Priority for Predictability

This Basic Priority picture shows that the higher from the midline that the **S** plotting point lies, the greater the intensity of the high **S** type in the person's style. The higher the intensity of the high **S** type, the more comfortable the person is in maintaining **Predictability** by keeping a *routine* in a comfortable, non-threatening, unchanging, stable environment. **S**s like sticking with what works. They prefer to maintain predictability. If pushed too hard, they will stubbornly, quietly resist change!

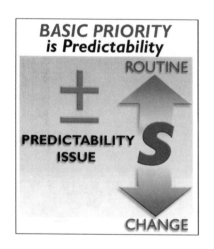

People on the low side of the **S** priority, away from the midline, tend to be more comfortable with change. Routine is boring to them, instead of comforting. They prefer to see **Predictability** as an opportunity to *change* their environment. They enjoy variety. They prefer to be spontaneous. If given the option, they will decide to try something different.

Do you place more importance in your decisions on sticking with what is already working or on the possibility of trying something new? These are the two factors in the **S** Basic Priority for predictability. If **S** is the highest type in your Style Blend, you will probably find that keeping things on an even keel is most important in any decision you make. If, on the other hand, you have a very low **S** type in your style, you will be more prone to suggest trying something new or different, just to see what happens. What a difference this can make!

A Priority for Procedure

This Basic Priority picture shows that the higher from the midline that the **C** plotting point lies, the greater the intensity of the high **C** type in the person's style. The higher the intensity of the high **C** type, the more comfortable the person is in using **Procedure** according to *facts* in an environment with well-defined structure. High **C**s want lots of facts and information in defined order. Things must be organized so that everyone plays by the rules! They prefer to uphold principles. If given the option, they will objectively decide on the correct procedure!

People on the low side of the **C** priority, away from the midline, are less comfortable in a rigid structure with strict rules. They prefer to use **Procedure** according to their *feelings* in an environment where they are free and independent. They prefer self-expression. If something touches their feelings, they will decide instinctively and subjectively, according to those feelings.

Do you place more importance in your decisions on the rules, facts and structure involved in a situation; or do you tend to go with your gut reaction? These are the two factors in the **C** Basic Priority for Procedure. If **C** is the highest type in your Style Blend, you will probably find that upholding principles through structure and order is most important in any decision you make. If, on the other hand, you have a very low **C** type in your style, you will be more prone to listen to your instincts and go with your feelings about your decision. What a difference this can make!

Which of these Basic Priorities is most important to you as you make a decision? As you review the Basic Priority charts we just learned, remember to observe the high perspectives of each style as well as the low perspectives. You may find that you favor several different aspects of the high or the low perspective in each Basic Priority. Which is the most important priority to you in making a decision? That's for you to decide! You may find that as you become more aware of your tendencies in this part of your personality, you are able to evaluate all these priorities in your decision. After all, isn't it important to consider the power you and others have in a situation? What about both logically evaluating the issues and also persuading the people involved in a decision? Don't we need to sometimes keep things running smoothly to maintain predictability, while at other times, we should start over or try something new? And finally, what procedure will we follow: are we bound by rules and structure or our own feelings when we decide? A good decision really considers all of these possibilities, while weighing the importance of each for the individual situation.

In life, we make many decisions every day. The issues usually involved in those choices call for balancing our priorities instead of choosing between them. We call upon our strengths under control to keep things in balance. Maybe this is why we can feel like life is one big juggling act! Our lives are more secure when we are confident in the decisions we make, and understanding ourselves is basic to finding this satisfaction.

We hope that your self-awareness grows as you begin to understand yourself through your personality style! This is the first step in the four steps to raising your **PQ**. Step one, *Learning to Understand Yourself*, is foundational to the next three steps. By the way... your **PQ** is showing!

Chapter Eight

Understanding Another Person

PQ Step Two

The second step in raising your *PQ* is to take what you have learned about yourself and expand your insights to include another person. In the last chapter, we discussed your Style Blend — the blending of traits from all four **DISC** types that make up your unique personality style. We became aware that no one is purely a **D**, **I**, **S** or **C**. Instead, each person is a unique style blend of these four basic types. In the same manner that you became aware of your own behavior and personality style, you can enhance your awareness of those around you. In these **DISC** types, you can find keys to understanding your spouse, child, friend, co-worker or business associate. These keys can unlock the doors to a more fulfilling personal relationship or a more successful business relationship!

You can begin to understand others by exploring how other personality styles have different perspectives, attitudes and preferences from your style. It is easy to understand someone who is a lot like us. However, for those who are not like us, we find the differences frequently drive us crazy! If you can become aware of the patterns in the behavior of others and see the merit of their perspective, you can *understand* what they do and perhaps learn to appreciate them more! They may simply see life from a different perspective than you do!

Look back at the charts in the previous chapter, and take note of the *Outlook on Life, Focus, Ideal Environment* and B*asic Needs* that you *did not* choose as your own. These will describe a very different perspective than your own choices described. For example, when I talk to Carl Smith, the Director of our Training Program, about a work project, I may be in a hurry to drive it through to completion as quickly as possible. I sometimes get too excited and tend to "run over" people in the process. I must remember that Carl's focus, as a high **S**, will be to provide excellent service to help everyone, while avoiding conflict at any cost. When Carl feels a conflict is occurring, he quietly "closes down" and stops working. By understanding how I can better relate to Carl, I am put in a position to interact in a more positive way with him and with his personality style. This helps both of us to be more productive and less stressed out. How we relate to, interact with, and react to another person with his or her personality style is called our *Combination*.

You may already have thought about someone close to you as you have read these **DISC** chapters. For instance, *you* may not be naturally **S**upportive, but your *spouse* really is! Or you are just *sure* that your boss is a high **I**, because he can even make work seem like fun! Or perhaps you recognized your **D**ominant child who seems to have a talent for pushing the limits at school. Sometimes you can observe the behavior of another person to gain clues about his or her personality style. As you learn about another person, you can be aware of things that person does that you need and appreciate. You may also be aware of things that person does that drives you crazy! We can learn about these Combinations and enjoy better relationships.

Your spouse or a close friend may be willing to show you the graphs in his or her *Adult Profile Assessment* or his or her personalized computer report. When you know the high type(s) in his or her style, you can refer to these charts for insights into that person's *Outlook, Focus, Ideal Environment* and *Basic Needs*. You will begin to be aware that his or her perspective is like yours, or that it is different from your perspective. You will begin to understand that how a person behaves, and how a person expresses something, is often a result of that person's personality perspective. You will then *see* through that person's eyes, and you will be able to understand him or her better. This is the beginning of *Step Two – Understanding Another Person*.

Combinations

We find *Combinations* in all areas of our lives. (Combinations refer to two or more people interacting with one another.) Marriage, friendship, co-workers, classmates, parent and child, teacher and student, brothers and sisters, employer and employee are all combinations that are part of long-term relationships. We also find combinations in short-term relationships with acquaintances, customers, salespersons and others with whom we interact in the course of daily living. How do we relate to these people? How do they relate to us?

As we relate to our spouse in our marriage relationship, we interact in Combinations. Almost every marriage relationship combination begins happily. After all, why would you marry someone you didn't like? Most of us marry someone we love deeply, with whom we plan to spend the rest of our lives. We usually appreciate characteristics about our mate that we don't have, and we like how different they are from us . As we interact and the relationship grows, a strange thing happens. We find characteristics in our mate that irritate us. We have discovered the truth that *opposites attract...then they attack!* Our differences create disharmony, and we become frustrated. How many times have you wondered, *"Why can't you be normal, like me?"* We need to remember that the very attractions that began our relationship were our differences. We also need to learn to appreciate our individual strengths and deal with our differences effectively. We need to understand how to live in Combination.

Living in Combination with our mate is one kind of personal relationship. We also have relationships that are professional relationships. In those Combinations, the main focus is working together. Why is it difficult for most couples to work together? Why do co-workers find it difficult to date? These Combinations create different dynamics! Our awareness of personality styles can help us understand the dynamics of these different Combinations and learn to develop more effective relationships in both areas of our lives.

As we learn about Combinations, remember that through our unique strengths, we enrich and support one another. As we become aware of our differences, they can become barriers to understanding and intimacy, or they can be bridges to awareness and growth. It depends on what we do with them!

Combinations- with the Dominant Type

High **D**s naturally take charge in a relationship. They take quick action when they recognize an opportunity to do something, and they can make sure that you gain full advantage from your opportunities as well. High **D**s quickly respond to the opportunity to try something new and tend to direct others to do the same!

Life is constantly changing, and high **D**s deal well with change. They often create change to get the results they want. We respect their problem-solving ability and draw on their strength to help us get through the difficulties in any situation.

For **D**ominant style people, a good relationship is one in which they have freedom from controls or supervision. They want to experience many varied activities with you, so your relationship will probably center around doing things they want to do and accomplishing their goals. They really enjoy a challenge, and they want to have authority and power to meet a challenge. You will feel the strength of their drive!

Ds expect aggressiveness in others. An argument to you is usually a discussion to them! They naturally evaluate you based on the results you achieve, and they are attracted to people who help them get things done. Personal friends usually provide them with fun, stability or expertise in an area of interest to them. They are interested in working with people who do the parts of a job that they don't have time to do.

Ds in Personal Relationships

with a **D** – This is a dynamic personal relationship. They do many different things together and usually are attracted to each other because they both like to get things done!

with an **I** – This is an exciting personal relationship. These two fast-paced people find stimulating challenges to experience.

with an **S** – This is a more difficult personal relationship, because of their contrasting styles. The **S** can offer steadiness and warmth to the **D**. The **S** is a practical help to the **D**, as well.

with a **C** – This is a very difficult personal relationship, because they both want to accomplish tasks. **D**s like to take risks and make adjustments as they go, while **C**s like to comply with rules and make a plan before they start! Since both perspectives are valuable, they can learn a lot from each other.

Ds in Professional Relationships

with a **D** – This is a competitive, professional relationship. If they have separate areas of control, they can work together effectively and will respect each other for the jobs they do.

with an **I** – This is a difficult professional relationship, because their work habits collide. When persuading others is part of the job, the **I** can give the **D** a more friendly approach.

with an **S** – This is an excellent professional relationship if the **D** is the co-worker or manager, because the **D** loves to start a project and the **S** loves to finish it!

with a **C** – This is a manageable professional relationship. They bring different skills to a project, and they both focus on the task. They will need to negotiate deadlines and quality expectations.

Combinations- with the Inspiring Type

The high *I* naturally makes a relationship loads of fun. Conversations with the inspiring type are stimulating, because *I*s are so expressive and full of life! As a high *I*, I love to go to lunch with a different staff member every day. I try to make the meal a fun treat with interesting conversation. The *I* type's enthusiasm is contagious, and everyone has a good time no matter what you do.

Life is constantly changing, and high *I*s welcome change. They know life is full of surprises and exciting things to do. And you will always be doing something exciting with them! People are naturally drawn to them, so you will seldom be alone with a high *I*. *I*s really are quite impressive in front of a group, where we can see and respect their ability to entertain and persuade others.

For *I*nspiring people, a good relationship is one in which they have freedom from a set schedule and from the responsibility for details. They really enjoy flexibility, and they love surprises more than any other type. They want social recognition and love to be popular with many people. They love to be the star of the show, and they really want to be a star to you. They can say the most amazing things, and they want the freedom to tell you how they feel about almost anything. *I*s make you feel like they are your best friend, and you are theirs.

*I*s expect flexibility in others. A scheduled appointment to you is usually a tentative arrangement to them! They naturally evaluate you based on your verbal skills, and they are attracted to people who present themselves and their ideas well. Personal friends usually provide them with focus, stability or expertise in an area of interest to them. They are interested in working with people who do the parts of a job that they feel are boring to do.

*I*s in Personal Relationships

with a **D** – This is an exciting personal relationship. Their fast-paced challenges are stimulated by sheer fun.

with an **I** – This is an incredible personal relationship. These two stars make life a grand surprise party!

with an **S** – This is a comfortable personal relationship, because of their love for people. The **I** can offer expressiveness and trust to the **S**. The **I** has an outgoing nature that helps the **S** feel comfortable when trying new things.

with a **C** – This is a very difficult personal relationship, because they have contrasting styles. The **I** offers excitement and fun, while the **C** likes to keep things consistent and structured. Since both perspectives are valuable, they can learn a lot from each other.

*I*s in Professional Relationships

with a **D** – This is a difficult professional relationship, because they have different priorities. Nevertheless, the **D** can give the **I** the focus needed to accomplish the great dreams that the **I** has!

with an **I** – This is an impulsive professional relationship. They both want recognition for their work, and they don't like to share the limelight! If they are popular together, they love each other, but in their flexibility, they may miss a logical plan to get the job done!

with an **S** – This is an excellent professional relationship. The **I** loves to create a dream, and the **S** loves to make it practical for people so that the dream can come true!

with a **C** – This is a manageable professional relationship. They play different roles in a project, and both roles are vital. One creates, and the other improves. They both love to work with ideas, concepts and theories.

Combinations- with the Supportive Type

The high **S** is naturally **S**upportive in a relationship. **S**s are relaxed and willing to do what you need. They are like anchors. They simply stay in one place, so that they will be there for you when you turn to them for help or companionship. I heavily depend on Carl Smith, our high **S** Director of Training at Personality Insights, to help make people comfortable at our conferences. People are naturally drawn to him, and they enjoy his companionship.

Life is constantly changing, but high **S**s remain the same. Because they are patient with others, high **S**s allow for your mistakes and forgive your human frailties. And who doesn't make mistakes? They are faithful and enduring. They develop deep and lasting relationships with their family members and a few close friends. They naturally think about what could have happened and give the other person the benefit of the doubt. We respect their reliability, and we depend on their loyalty to help us get through the difficulties of life.

To a **S**upportive style person, a good relationship is one based on sincere appreciation for one another. Kind words of appreciation come easily to **S**s, and they need your appreciation in return. They are most comfortable within the boundaries of routine, for they like sticking with what works. They seem to enjoy simply being with you. Your relationship will probably center on doing things you enjoy, as long as they don't have to try something alone that is too new or too risky. They are happiest and at ease within the stability of their home and family. Perhaps more than any other type, they will protect harmonious family relationships. They work best in situations where they are allowed time to adjust to change, because they want to feel comfortable with what is going to happen. They also want to be sure that predictable results can be expected, and that everyone is prepared for the adjustment. With this security established, you will feel the strength of their support!

Ss expect friendliness in others. They really don't enjoy disagreement or sarcastic words! They naturally evaluate you by your consistency, and they are attracted to people who are unpretentious and honest. Personal friends usually provide them with introductions, involvement or expertise in an area of interest to them. They are interested in working with people who take the risk to get the job started and then rely on them to help with the routine.

Ss in Personal Relationships

with a **D** – This is a more difficult personal relationship because of their contrasting styles. The **D** can offer determination and initiative to the **S**. The **D** is a practical director for the **S**, as well.

with an **I** – This is a comfortable personal relationship, because of their love for people. The **S** can offer steadiness and support to the **I**. The **S** has an appreciative nature that helps the **I** feel the approval he or she needs to try a new task.

with an **S** – This is an easy personal relationship, because they are both supportive and loyal. They love to be together and seek harmony with one another above all else.

with a **C** – This is a proper, yet personal, relationship. They respect the rights and privacy of the other person. They don't intrude on one another. The **S** extends kindness, loyalty and acceptance to the **C** in a way that the **C** can receive and respect.

Ss in Professional Relationships

with a **D** – This is a working professional relationship when the **S** is manager, but only if the **D** respects the authority and decision-making style of the **S** manager. The **S** can be a very practical and patient manager for the driving **D**, who can benefit from the experience of the **S**.

with an **I** – This is an excellent professional relationship. The **S** is patient with the impulsive high **I**, who loves to involve the high **S** in whatever is being done.

with an **S** – This is a consistent professional relationship. They naturally fall into a practical routine and develop a friendly working relationship. They will complete tasks with teamwork and cooperation.

with a **C** – This is a proper professional relationship with a friendly face. The **S** will use the theories and analysis of the **C** to provide routine procedures. This will ensure consistent quality performance and products.

Combinations- with the Cautious Type

High **C**s naturally fulfill their proper role in a relationship. They follow the instructions in everything they do. This includes understanding and maintaining their role with you. They want to understand your expectations. **C**s will work tirelessly to fulfill their own expectations and role in your relationship. They will often ask questions of you, checking for accuracy in their requirements and yours. "Do you need me to go over this information one more time before we go to press?" is a common question from Beth McLendon, our high **C** book editor. You see, she is checking to see if she has completed her role in preparing our materials for printing. We depend on her attention to detail in order to produce quality products which will give our customers their best value!

Life is constantly changing, and high **C**s guard against impulsive or abrupt changes. They want to reduce the risks involved with change by developing guidelines for untried theories. They will experiment to test for accuracy and will validate their information with experts for factual reassurance. We respect their specialized ability. We draw on their expertise and cool logic to help us solve the dilemmas in any situation.

To a **C**autious style person, a good relationship is one in which he or she has a proper role and a polite understanding with the other person. **C**s want factual reassurances without illogical or impulsive emotions to handle. Your relationship will probably center on doing things related to a mutual area of interest or field of study. They like to be part of a group or club. They really enjoy excellence in workmanship or artistic endeavors, both as an observer and as an artisan, themselves. They can take hours analyzing an idea, work of art or design. They are intensely unique individuals, and you will feel the strength of their quest for excellence!

Cs expect everyone to play by the rules. They expect you to live by precise standards, and they also expect themselves to live by precise standards! They naturally evaluate you based on the accuracy you maintain, and they are attracted to people who do things with excellence. Personal friends usually provide them with challenge, involvement or acceptance. They are interested in working with people who allow them to express and develop their specialized ability.

Cs in Personal Relationships

with a **D** – This is a very difficult personal relationship, because they both want to accomplish tasks. The **C** requires thoroughness, excellence and accuracy, while the **D** demands pioneering and risk-taking to derive adventure and ambition. Since both perspectives are valuable, they can learn a lot from each other.

with an **I** – This is a very difficult personal relationship, because they have contrasting styles. The **C** thinks about rules and roles in the relationship, while the **I** wants to feel excitement in a relationship where there is freedom to explore the world and express his or her feelings. Since both perspectives are valuable, they can learn a lot from each other.

with an **S** – This is a proper, yet personal, relationship. They respect the rights and privacy of the other person. They don't intrude on one another. The **C** recognizes the predictability and appreciates the patience of the **S**. This gives a secure role to the **S** in a way that the **S** can receive and respect.

with a **C** – This is a proper relationship. They are both careful to understand and fulfill their role for the other in a personal relationship. Because of their sensitivity, they can learn how to meet the needs of the other and will work on the relationship to continue to improve it.

Cs in Professional Relationships

with a **D** – This is a manageable professional relationship. They bring different skills to a project, and they both focus on the task. They will need to negotiate accountability and responsibility.

with an **I** – This is a manageable professional relationship. They play different roles in a project, and both roles are vital. The **C** establishes the validity of cold, hard facts, and the **I** expresses feelings that relate those facts to people. The **I** is inspired with an intuition, or gut instinct. The **C** describes, defines and validates a theory that generalizes the intuition and makes it useful to others.

with an **S** – This is an amiable professional relationship with defined roles. The **S** will provide the sensitivity to people, while the **C** will provide specialized and accurate information. This will ensure positive outcomes. Together they will provide quality products and services. In short, what they do will work easily and be right every time!

with a **C** – This is a responsible professional relationship. They take their roles seriously and require similar high standards. They will often develop different areas of expertise and will work well together on projects where they can validate each other's work.

Good Combinations and Making Combinations Good

As you have read each of these sections about **DISC** types in Combinations, you have found some Combinations of types that are naturally easier, while others are more difficult to manage.

We all have some relationships that are easy most of the time; these are good Combinations for us. We also have some relationships that require a lot of work to make them good or a lot of good will to make them work! This is what we mean by making Combinations good. We can make almost any Combination good if we seek to understand each other, recognize our own needs and learn how to meet the needs of the other person.

Understanding your personality style, with your strengths and struggles, and becoming aware of another person's style, with the strengths and struggles of your unique styles in Combination, empowers your possibilities for great relationships! You are taking great strides in raising your **PQ**!

Chapter Nine

Adapting Your Style

PQ Step Three

Awareness and Understanding for Better Relationships

As you become aware of another person's style, you will begin to see your differences in a different light. *Step Three: Adapting Your Style to Create Better Relationships* means using your awareness of the other person to understand his or her needs. You can begin to exercise your ability to communicate effectively and to act intelligently by adapting your words and actions to the style of the other person, so that you can meet his or her needs. Simply put, this means that, instead of giving someone else what *you* need, you give that person what *he or she* needs in order to truly communicate better. This is also known as the Platinum Rule. The Golden Rule says, "Do unto others as you would have them do unto you." However, the Platinum Rule says, "Do unto others as they actually need you to do unto them." In other words, the Platinum Rule is more about treating others the way *they* want and need to be treated, not the way *you* want to be treated – without being phony or underhanded.

A Personal Example

How do I and my Administrative Assistant, Cindy, do this? When Cindy meets with me to work on a project, I try to remember to allow her time to talk about what's going on at the moment - especially as it relates to all of her work. I give her my attention and listen to her carefully as we review where we are in our workload. Because she has so much to do, I try to help her pace herself with her work by asking her questions concerning how to proceed with current projects. Allowing her flexibility gives her the freedom she needs to focus her attention on urgent projects and work, and yet encourages her to communicate her own ideas on current projects. We make room for the needs of the other person. This enables each of us to be comfortable and open to communicate and work together. This sounds friendly and polite, *and* it is!

Adapting our styles is even more important when we feel that the other person is doing something just to drive us crazy! It requires understanding our different personality styles and exercising more self-control through intelligent choices. We have to *think* before we *act!*

When our Staff Editor, Jim Benton, a high **D** style, *is driving* to get the wording on a project consistently correct, I often feel a little uncomfortable. As a high **I** style, I may feel like telling a *funny* story to lighten the mood, but I don't. Instead, I take a deep breath and come up with another *choice* for wording that we both feel is *correct*. I make room for his *drive* for *correctness* because I respect his ability to produce *concise clarity*. Sometimes my high **I** style gets me distracted from getting to a project, but Jim's high **D** style helps me to stay focused. He doesn't get irritated and begin to push me. He chooses to remember that a high **I** sometimes gets sidetracked telling stories to someone or talking to a friend at lunch. If I get sidetracked, Jim finds another project to work on until I return. Jim values my storytelling and my conversation skills. He realizes that they help me to entertain as I explain **DISC** information in seminars and in our resource materials. Jim knows that these abilities are the reason why our resources are so popular and effective.

We recognize that barriers to effective interaction are thrown up naturally because of our different perspectives. We can break down the barriers and build bridges of understanding when we value the other person, our relationship and our different perspectives. This is the real basis for Step Three. If you are Task-oriented, you need to find value in people. If you are People-oriented, you need to remember how important it is to complete your tasks. Watch for the good that comes when an Outgoing person reaches out to you. See how important a Reserved manner is when uncovering and correcting mistakes. Adapting your style to have better relationships will be easier when you can really appreciate, understand and value a perspective that is different from your own.

Predictable Patterns, not Personality Boxes

Psychologist Alfred Adler said, "I don't put people in boxes; I just keep finding them there." Putting anyone in a personality box is pointless, because each person has some traits from each personality style. People also have the power of self-awareness. They have the ability to make choices about how they respond in an environment or how they relate in a relationship. But *DISC*overing their predominant type can really help us begin to mind our *P*s and *Q*s:

Prize his or her personality perspective.

Quietly satisfy his or her style needs.

Prepare your thoughts and feelings to relate to him or her.

Quickly break down barriers and build bridges of communication between us.

Building the Bridges in Your Style Blend

Jim Benton (a high *D*) and I (a high *I*) have a professional relationship that we described earlier as sometimes challenging. Jim is task-oriented; I am people-oriented. Yet we make it work by building bridges of communication. How can we do this? One of our secrets lies in the secondary types in our style blends. Jim has a high *C* in his style blend, but he also has enough *I* to be a little mischievous. This means that he can be flexible in relating to me, because he enjoys the fun we share. I, for my part, have *S* above the midline as well. This means that I can be sensitive to Jim's need for support in working toward our goals. These more flexible types in each of our styles can help us build bridges of understanding and appreciation. You can see how personal relationships can become complex very quickly! Becoming aware of the tendencies within your style blend can give you the understanding you need to make choices for building better relationships.

Assumptions and Expectations

Even when we do everything in our power to make good choices in our relationships, there are times when we seem to do everything wrong. We hurt those close to us, even when we have the best of intentions. The secret to this problem often lies in the assumptions or expectations that we bring to a relationship. When we assume that the other person feels or thinks the way we do, we are often surprised to find that this is not the case. We should not be disappointed with these differences. Ruth Bell Graham, when asked if she and husband, Billy Graham had similar personalities, replied, "Of course not – I'm nothing like him. But after all, if two people are just alike... all the time... about everything... one of them is unnecessary!" How insightful to expect differences!

Protecting a Relationship

One of the differences in personalities that frequently causes pain in our relationships is our natural fears. This is an area where the other person can push you out of control or put up a barrier between you. Protecting the other person by being sensitive to his or her fears can build a bridge to a stronger relationship. Simply exposing another's vulnerability can put up a barrier that only weakens, or even kills, a relationship. We need to understand one another's fears, so we can protect our relationships!

*DISC*overing our Fears

Secret Fears

D	...*Being taken advantage of*
★	...*Loss of social recognition*
S	...*Change; Confrontation*
C	...*Irrational acts; The unknown or the uncertain*

High **D**s focus on achieving their goals and overcoming obstacles. However, they will walk away from interaction or a relationship that takes advantage of them. They want to win *with* you, but if they perceive that you are taking advantage of their power or using them for your own purposes, they may turn their efforts toward making you lose! They will then react with hot anger. If they cannot make you lose, they will still go to great lengths to get even, and frequently, they just drop out of a relationship completely.

High **I**s feel that there is nothing worse than public embarrassment. They fear the loss of social recognition and popularity. If you make them look bad in front of a group, they may overreact with a flood of emotions meant to blame someone else for the embarrassment or to make you look ridiculous. In the heat of the moment, they can say hurtful words that deeply wound your relationship.

High **S**s avoid confrontation at all costs. If you surprise them with immediate changes, they will probably feel threatened and vulnerable, but they usually reserve and conceal these feelings. Instead of reacting toward you, they just shut down and may find escape in excessive sleep. Beneath their superficial indifference, they can build a mighty barrier of grudges that are difficult to uncover. These grudges can strangle your relationship.

High **C**s think that irrational acts are the sign of an unprincipled person. Principles are vital for them, so they may insist on an explanation that is followed closely by more rational behavior from you. They keep their feelings under control. Any indication of antagonism from you will make them withdraw from you. They may not ask for a second explanation but will instead protect themselves with time alone and by building an invisible, cold wall between you and them. This icy barrier can freeze a real relationship between you.

A Better Response to Stress

How can we avoid these difficult and sometimes deadly relationship barriers? How can we protect the people we love and the people who work with us? First, we can learn to adapt to the styles of others and to protect others by being sensitive to their fears. Next, we can build bridges to stronger relationships. When we are aware of our own fear reactions, we can do what we need to do for recovery and choose to respond more effectively. Anger is a common fear reaction that really gets our attention. We need to discover the fear or hurt that usually lurks behind it. Most high **D** types know that when they get stressed and then get angry, they should find something to do that is unrelated to what made them upset. Also, if a person has a lot of **C** in him or her, it will give that person some time to think about what was behind the anger in the first place. Then the person can usually make sense of the situation, regain control and decide on a plan of action to take care of the problem. This is much more effective than the natural reaction of cutting someone to shreds with hostile words!

Activities *DISC* Types Need to Recover under Stress

High **D**s need physical activity to recover under stress. This may mean going for a walk or getting some exercise in a favorite sport. It may also mean doing some kind of work that is very different from their everyday job - like straightening the garage or cleaning out the attic. Many high **D**s like to work in their yard to relieve stress or tension.

High **I**s need social activity to help them recover under stress. This may mean going out with friends to dinner or a movie. It may also mean calling a friend simply to unwind and talk. For example, I like to go to lunch in my red convertible with different staff members. It feels like we are making progress while we talk! Every day it seems like there is a new adventure around our office!

High **S**s need undirected activity to recover under stress. This may mean "piddling" around the house or watching a movie they have seen over and over. Carl Smith, Director of our Training Program, has several favorite movies. He explains that he feels better when he sees the happy ending. He feels relieved and then recovers. For another **S**, it may mean sitting around doing nothing in particular.

Mark Wagnon is our Consultant Care Specialist, and he is a high **S** type. He relieves stress by going for a long ride on his motorcycle. Mark says, "Riding my motorcycle has no structure. Just being out in the wind and sun helps me to feel calm and peaceful. When I am riding my motorcycle with other bikers, we feel like a family. We always wave at each other and experience a sense of connection while we ride." (When I heard Mark explain this, I was a little surprised. That is not what I pictured a biker thinking. But, then I realized my mental picture of most bikers was that of a group of "Hell's Angels".... definitely not a bunch of high **S** types!)

High **C**s need cognitive activity to recover under stress. This may mean reading a magazine or story. It may also mean putting together a puzzle or playing solitaire. I know one high **C** math whiz that likes to do calculus problems to unwind!

Whatever your style, find an activity that helps you to unwind. Make sure it is one that is readily available when you need it. You may love to unwind on a sailboat, but if you live too far from the ocean or a lake, you may need to find something else you enjoy! Remember to make allowances for others to unwind. We can all learn to be more forgiving towards ourselves and others when we get stressed out!

Reinforcing our Relationships

No matter how much we care or how hard we try, there are times in every relationship when we need to reinforce our relationship and give the gift of encouragement to one another. Secure relationships make our days satisfying and our lives significant. We all want to make our world a better place. We can encourage others with words and actions, and we can **DISC**over how to give others what they need instead of what we need as encouragement.

High **D**s receive encouraging words that are direct and to the point. Use a confident, firm tone, and be brief. Let them know how they have solved a significant problem. Tell them how their results satisfied an important need for you. Reward them for reaching their goals with a gift related to their achievement or with something you know that they really want. If you have the power to do so, reinforce their responsibility by giving them appropriate authority. Recognize their dynamic leadership if they are in authority over you. In this way, you can encourage them and reinforce your positive relationship with them.

High *I*s receive encouraging words that are friendly, positive and informal. Use an excited tone, and don't be afraid to express your feelings to them. Let them know how impressed you are. Tell them who else recognized the significance of what they did. Share with them how what they did strengthened your relationship with them. Give them a pat on the back or an appropriate smile and hug. They will be encouraged by your touch or closeness. If you have the position to do it, reinforce their responsibility by giving them appropriate public recognition. Encourage their inspiring leadership by speaking well of them to others within your common circles of influence. In this way, you can encourage them and reinforce your positive relationship with them.

High **S**s receive encouraging words that are sincere, kind and personal. Use a relaxed and gentle tone, and be friendly. Let them know how satisfied you are. Tell them how they really helped you and strengthened your relationship with them. Give them a sentimental memento or offer to do some small service for them that would cost you little but would really please them. They will be encouraged by your act of service for them, especially if it is not given in front of others. If you have the relationship with them to do it, reinforce their responsibility by making an allowance for the needs of their family. You could also offer your personal, nonverbal acceptance and assurances to them. Appreciate their servant leadership with quiet support. In this way, you can encourage them and reinforce your positive relationship with them.

High **C**s receive encouraging words that are accurate and unemotional. Use a patient, yet persistent tone, for they may correct your assessment of their work or reject your flattery of their person. Let them know how serious you are. Specifically tell them how significant you think their contribution was for you and your relationship with them. Give them your attention by planning and inviting them to a nice dinner or to an excellent movie. They will be encouraged when you spend some quality time with them. Reinforce their responsibility by expanding their role, if possible. Write them a letter using carefully chosen words recording their responsible leadership and example. In this way, you can encourage them and reinforce your positive relationship with them.

Strengthen Your Relationships

DISC is not a scientific formula, but it is predictable patterns of behavior. Your intentions and efforts to apply this information will do much to break down barriers and build bridges that will strengthen your relationships. As your self-awareness grows, your understanding of your actions and attitudes in your relationships becomes clearer. As you begin to focus your attention on other people, you can learn about their fears and their needs and how to encourage them in their style. You are laying a strong foundation to empower your relationships. Watch out for your **PQ**, because now we know that *You've Got Style!*

Chapter Ten

Building Better Teams

PQ Step Four

Awareness and Understanding for Teamwork

As we begin the twenty-first century, technology has *dissolved* the distance barrier to communication. We can use e-mail to send an instant message almost anywhere in the world. We can now explore more information on the Internet than most people in the past had available to them over their entire lives. At the same time, technology has sometimes *increased* the distance barriers to effective communication. There is something about seeing a person's face, hearing a response, and talking to someone in person that simply cannot be simulated with our modern technology. Remember the last time that you got a recording on a telephone response system? No matter how hard the voice on the machine tried to communicate with you, talking to a machine is just not the same as talking to a person, *in person!*

Technology is a great tool for us to use, but we still need personal contact, successful personal interaction and an individual relationship. We may love high tech, but we still need high touch!

Now you might think that all this quick communication would give us more time for our relationships, but the opposite seems to be true. Time is a different thing to us than it was to our grandparents. While relationships are just as valuable today as they were to our grandparents, we tend to see less of one another. We save time by using forms of instant communication that do not require us to be together. As the speed of our personal lives increases and business goes increasingly electronic, we must become more skilled at developing our people skills. The time we spend developing personal and business relationships must be used effectively.

Relationships are important to each of us, because we are human, and we want our lives to be significant. We want the security of family relationships in which we encourage each other to grow and enjoy life together. We also want to work together and be successful. In our personal and professional lives, we want the satisfaction of playing our part in something bigger than ourselves. We find this through our faith in God, ourselves and the people we love. We find this in our relationships with others and in what we do. Sometimes we find that working together in a group brings the best results. This group becomes a *team*, and a special relationship develops within a true team.

A true team is formed when two or more people interact freely and personally to accomplish something together. Interacting freely means that team members accept one another and are comfortable with one another. They feel secure so that they do not protect or filter their contributions. They interact personally, knowing that the other team members will not attack them, because each person in the group values their contributions. Within the framework of this interaction, the team synergy accomplishes something greater than any one team member alone might do. This is how *Together Everyone Achieves More*!

Whether in our family or a work group, we want to find the magic created when we become part of a team. A team is a group of players working together that creates something better than any one of them alone could create. That something, whether an atmosphere for the individual development of the team members or a tangible product, comes from *teamwork*.

Family teamwork creates an atmosphere and is a life-changing experience. It produces growing individuals who have healthy relationships. Your life would not be the same if you had a different father or mother. Your life is probably deeply affected by your brothers and sisters, as well. Think for a moment about your family. Now try to imagine what your family might have been like if one person were removed. If you picked your least favorite family member, you might be thinking, "Great! I'd love to be without him!"

On the other hand, if you picked the person closest to you, you might wonder how you would ever have lived without that person! In either case, you can see how each person makes a unique contribution to your family. Your family is the first team in which you belonged, because you were born into it!

Other teams come and go throughout your life. Remember summer camp when you were a child? You can easily remember the magic of bonding with your cabin mates and becoming a team. You played together and worked together, and when camp was finished, it was never the same again. Things changed. You changed. But you would love to step back into that special team, if you could. As an adult, you have probably worked on various teams. Teamwork, on a professional project, creates an atmosphere to produce goods or services that improve the quality of life for everyone. Often a work team is successful when the individual parts, or persons, would have failed alone. It is a special experience, and we love to see the results!

In any kind of team, whether family or work, different personality types make different contributions to the team. As we are aware of our own perspective and recognize the perspectives of other people on the team, we can learn to respect each other and work together to satisfy the requirements of the team's work. This includes meeting the individual needs of the team members, as well as achieving balance through the contributions of everyone involved. This is the basis of *PQ Step 4: Building Better Teams.*

Goal Setting

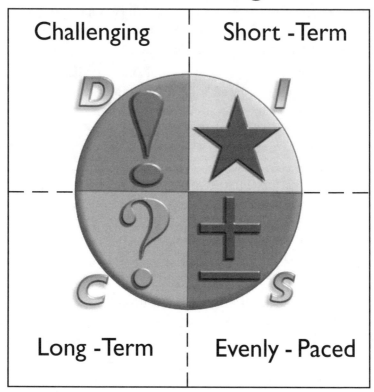

Challenging	Short -Term
Long -Term	Evenly - Paced

Goal Setting

Teamwork usually begins with setting goals for the team, so we will begin with awareness of differences in our approach to *setting goals*.

Goal setting is emphasized in our society today, and goal setting can be very easy for us to do. It is accomplishing those goals that presents the challenge! An archery target is huge compared to the tiny bull's eye in the center. Anyone can see the bull's eye, but understanding and developing your skill is what empowers you to hit the bull's eye. We all can write down goals, but as we understand our preferred approach, we can develop the type of strategy that empowers us to accomplish them, as well.

Ds are empowered by a challenging goal. Setting a very difficult goal energizes them! Let someone else do the easy part. It is not worth their effort. They like to set their own goals and achieve their own objectives.

Is live in the moment, so they need short-term goals with immediate rewards. The recognition they receive from a daily phone call may keep them working toward the goal better than a monthly meeting.

Be patient with **S**s by remembering "slow and steady wins the race." They will start slowly, so do not start with unrealistic goals. Once they start, however, they are good finishers! When they are comfortable, they will stick to a routine until they finish. Remember to give them the affirmation that they need along the way.

Cs are careful planners. They will first plan, and then they will set a realistic goal with long-term benefits. Their consistent, conscientious efforts will continue to empower them to reach their goal. They would really prefer to have all the details of their plan worked out in advance; sometimes this is impossible or impractical. If this causes them to get stuck, they may need your confidence to begin from where they are.

Each team member contributes a valuable perspective to setting goals for the team. We need long-range planning and short-term objectives. We also need someone who is willing to take the risk and get started, as well as someone to make sure that everyone on the team is comfortable with the plan and willing to contribute toward the goal. Effective goal setting includes all of us!

Task Method

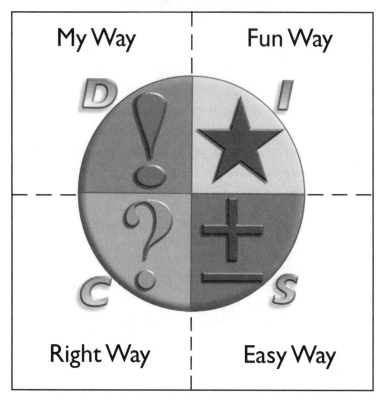

My Way	Fun Way
Right Way	Easy Way

Task Method

Once the team establishes its goals, each individual will approach his or her task very differently. Understanding and expecting these differences can help everyone on a team pull together using their strengths, instead of pulling apart and struggling. We have **DISC**overed that each type has a different task method.

Ds have confidence in conquering a task. They tend to lack self-doubt. They will decisively insist, "*My Way* is the best way to do it!"

*I*s find ways to make work fun and to involve people in everything they do. They love to shout, "This is the *Fun Way* to do it!"

*S*s will rehearse a plan in their mind until it feels friendly and comfortable. Then they work at a patient, steady pace until it is finished. They pat your arm and say, "Don't worry. We can do it together. This is the *Easy Way* to do it."

*C*s plan their work and then work their plan. They say, "I can show you the *Right Way* to do it."

Here is an example of an individual who recognized at an early age that there are different task methods:

My dad would often give my brother and me the same chore to finish at a certain time. When the time came, Dad would come back, and I would have the chore finished, but my brother would still be planning the right way to do it. I may not have done it the easiest or best way, but I did manage to get it done. I soon began to realize that talking to my (High C) brother before I started, would often make my (High D) work much easier. I could use his plan to speed up my work!

This individual understood that different styles have different strengths in their approach to their work. He learned to use his brother's strength in planning, along with his strength in doing. In the same way, we can recognize the importance of the pioneering **D** who forges ahead to get the job done. We can enjoy the inspiration of the *I* who makes us whistle while we work. We can appreciate the adaptability of the **S** who finds an easy way to accomplish the task. And we can respect the conscientiousness of the **C** who can develop a plan that can organize all our tasks in order to accomplish our goals!

*DISC*over Your Team Contributions

Wouldn't you love to discover how you can contribute your strengths to your team, while each team member is able to do the same? Just as a baseball team consists of more positions than the pitcher, your team will need the contributions of all four types for a well-rounded, strong team. Take a few minutes to consider these team strengths:

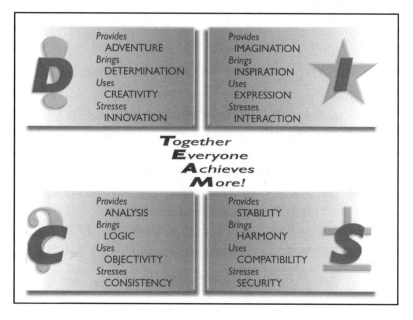

The Strength of the High **D** on the Team

High **D**s provide adventure. Their primary drive, the focus of their strength for the team, is to direct and control the efforts of the team. They ask, "What if we could do that...? I bet we could!" **D**s bring determination to the team. They contribute most effectively as innovative problem-solvers who face challenges as they come. They use creativity to change the challenges into energy directed at the goal. High **D**s stress innovation. **D**s are capable of handling many activities at once.

122

If you have a high D style: You are confident and decisive and may be bored by details. As a result, you may quickly change a plan of action to get the results you want. Your priority is power. You like new and innovative things and respond to challenges. Handling several issues at once energizes you. Your body language can be intimidating. You can be aggressive and demanding, and you will be naturally dominant in any setting. The secret to your effectiveness on a team is your awareness of and attention to the feelings of your team members, especially as you communicate your respect for their contributions to your team.

The Strength of the High *I* on the Team

High *I*s provide imagination. Their primary drive, the focus of their strength for the team, is to create a favorable, friendly environment that will enhance the efforts of the team. They ask, "Wouldn't it be fun if we could...? Just imagine that!" The *I*s bring spontaneity to the team. They contribute most effectively as magnetic energizers who inspire the team with their quick, affirming words and their expressive, optimistic feelings. High *I*s stress interaction and are capable of handling high profile assignments with people.

If you have a high *I* style: You are enthusiastic and persuasive, and you love being with people! You like to have fun and talk a lot. You are naturally inspiring and interesting, so talking about your team and its project will be easy for you. Your priority is people. You get people excited about what you are doing, so they love to come to you for encouragement. Your body language is animated and expressive, so your feelings are easily visible to others. Your mood may easily swing from elation to boredom. The secret to your effectiveness on a team is your awareness of, and attention to the need to follow-through on things. This will show your respect for the feelings of your team members and your respect for their contributions to your team.

The Strength of the High S on the Team

High Ss provide stability. Their primary drive, the focus of their strength for the team, is to create a supportive, secure environment for all the members of the team. They ask, "How could we do that...? If we help one another, I feel we would!" Ss bring harmony to the team and contribute most effectively to follow-through and completing a task. They are skilled at establishing practical routines, because they use compatibility to work along with their team members. High Ss stress security. They are capable of predictable and consistent support that minimizes conflict among team members.

If you have a high S style: You are steady and dependable, and people tend to trust you. You naturally invest yourself in others. You come alongside others to support and help in order to get consistent, practical results. Your priority is predictability. You are sympathetic and accepting. You like to help everyone be more comfortable with the team contributions they make. Your body language is warm and gentle. People may impose upon you too easily, because you don't want to create any conflict. You can be calm and amiable, and you will be naturally supportive in any setting. The secret to your effectiveness on a team is your awareness of, and attention to, the interdependence you develop with your team members, which can allow you to move quickly on problems and issues.

The Strength of the High C on the Team

High Cs provide analysis. Their primary drive, the focus of their strength for the team, is to be Cautious in order to do things correctly as a team. They ask, "Why should we do that...? I think perhaps we should!" Cs bring logic to the team and contribute most effectively as a validator of data. They are precise detail specialists who are diplomatic in addressing the complexities of an issue or idea. High Cs use objectivity to evaluate the excellence and quality of the work from the team. High Cs stress consistency. They are capable of exacting accuracy and structuring procedures for the team.

If you have a high C style: You enjoy planning and procedure, and you need to be organized. You look for order in life. You may discount feelings, because they do not easily fit into this paradigm. Your priority is procedure according to facts. You like high standards, and you are energized by excellence from your team members. You study facts and figures to validate information. Your body language may be cool and aloof. You can be intense and a perfectionist, so you will be naturally cautious in any setting. The secret of your effectiveness on a team is your awareness of, and attention to, the practical application of ideals and theories as the bigger focus for the team efforts. This will communicate your respect for your team members and their contributions to your team.

Bridging over the Challenges of Your Team

See how much we need one another? Even though we need each other, we still get on each other's nerves. Because handling irritations is so crucial to successful teamwork, we must also understand the role of conflict within a team. Think back to your childhood - either in your home or at camp. Did you ever fight with those team members? Fighting, or conflict, has a way of cementing our relationships. We set our bridges in stone, and we build our barriers in stone. Conflict arises from stress, and we have different ways of responding under pressure.

When high **D**s are under pressure, they will push. They push people to solve the problem, and they push themselves to resolve the situation. Under control, this can build a bridge where everyone attacks a problem together.

When high **I**s are under pressure, they will pull. They pull people along with them in a frenzy of activity, and they pull themselves into everyone's attention. Under control, this can build a bridge where everyone pulls together.

When high **S**s are under pressure, they will bend. They bend for people to avert conflict, and they bend themselves to accommodate the situation. Under control, this can build a bridge of acceptance.

When high **C**s are under pressure, they will stiffen. They stiffen the rules for people to resolve the issue, and they stiffen themselves to stay rigid in the situation. Under control, this can build a bridge of consistency over emotion.

Bridges of Communication for Your Team

Each type is vital to the effective interaction and accomplishments of a true team. Each team member needs to be able to recognize and respect the strengths and weaknesses of each team member. When we discover the truth of what we like and what we don't like, we often find out that the other types actually like what we don't like! At that point, it is a good idea to allow someone else to excel in that area. This is a great way to cooperate as a team. When each person is excelling in his or her own way, it strengthens the team!

Ds can ask the **I**s to...
- Create fun that brings the team together
- Talk with team members just to encourage them

Ds can ask the **S**s to...
- Perform routine tasks
- Complete projects

Ds can ask the **C**s to...
- Be responsible for details
- Track long-term critical analysis

Is can ask the Ds to...
- Make unpopular decisions
- Take the heat from those decisions

Is can ask the Ss to...
- Wait for someone
- Perform repetitive tasks

Is can ask the Cs to...
- Take care of the details
- Follow procedure, especially when it is inflexible

Ss can ask the Ds to...
- Take the risk by making the decision
- Deal with conflict directly

Ss can ask the Is to...
- Change directions on a moment's notice
- Speak in front of large groups

Ss can ask the Cs to...
- Decipher complex problems
- Conduct critical analysis

Cs can ask the Ds to...
- Confront people directly
- Make quick decisions

Cs can ask the Is to...
- Help with ideas
- Provide fun, spontaneous activities

Cs can ask the Ss to...
- Accommodate human imperfections
- Find a compromise for the sake of harmony

How does a true team work? It starts as you understand your gifts to the team and the gifts of each team member. You begin to see your differences in a different light. You respect the perspective of each team member as you set goals, accomplish tasks and contribute your special strengths to the team. You protect your team members as you bridge over their struggles and ask them to communicate their strengths to you. In essence, this means exercising your ability to communicate effectively and act intelligently by adapting your words and actions to the personality style of others. You *can* meet the needs of the individual team members, while you accomplish the objectives of the team as a whole.

Empowering You to Improve

We hope that these pages empower you to improve, through understanding yourself and others, so that you create better relationships and build better teams.

> *Life is a journey:*
>
> *adventure, excitement, routine and rules.*
>
> *Come along with us, and show the world that*
>
> ***You've Got Style!***